THANKSGIVING
IN AMERICA

THE LEGENDS AND THE PROCLAMATIONS

THANKSGIVING IN AMERICA

LYNN KELLER & LANCE KELLER

PRIMIX
PUBLISHING
THE WRITE CHOICE

Primix Publishing
485c US Highway 1 South
Suite 100
Iselin, NJ 08830
www.primixpublishing.com
Phone: 1-800-538-5788

Published by Primix Publishing: 09/19/2024

ISBN: 979-8-89194-298-1(sc)
ISBN: 979-8-89194-299-8(e)

CONTENTS

On the 401th ANNIVERSARY OF THANKSGIVING

In recognition to Robert Z Finkelstein, history professor extraordinaire, whose all too short time on Earth belies the enormity of his influence to those whom he mentored and befriended.

This book is also dedicated to our ancestors

The unsung heroes, the women in the Colony

Lynn's Mother, Anna Louise Smith, was a descendant of Mary Brewster, Constance Hopkins, and her Step-Mother Elizabeth Hopkins. In addition, Eleanor Billingsley, fits in our family. Other Mayflower ancestors

William Brewster, Stephen and Giles Hopkins.

The smallpox epidemic of 1623, deaths included President Obama's ancestor, Thomas Blossom, who became the leader of the John Robinson's congregation after his death. Our ancestors, who died then, were Priscilla Brewster, daughter of William and Mary Brewster, and Chief John Hyanno

Accurate genealogy led

PREFACE

America. Our Pilgrims came to America to be separated from the entire Thanksgiving story has nothing to do with Puritans in royalty as well as organized religion. They objected to King James, his version of the bible and religious bias. The Pilgrims, who were connected to Pastor John Robinson, came to the Plymouth area and the Cape from 1620 to 1629.

The Puritans were non-separatists. Many had direct ties to English Royalty and were generally wealthy. They were members of the Church of England but wanted to eliminate practices that mirrored Catholicism. They were intent in cutting ties with the Pope. They objected to King Charles L. Although he practiced noninterference in religion, he was heavy handed with taxation.

Charles I came to the throne in 1625. The Winthrop Fleet Puritans began arriving in 1628 and settled in the Boston Harbor and spread west and north. The Pilgrims and Puritans lived in separate territories, Pilgrims to the South and Puritans to the North. There were very few intermarriages in the early years. They were two distinct societies.

The Pilgrims were not expansionists. They "stayed with their own". The Pilgrims eventually evolved into Unitarians and Quakers whereas the Puritans founded mainstream Protestant religions. They each had very different relationships with the Wampanoag's.

Accurate genealogy is a boon to history. Every tale is illuminated by knowing the cast of characters deeply. Cross-checking lineage can clarify or eliminate theories and stories. Literally, the bonds of our fathers (and mothers) matter. For several generations, descendants of the Mayflower passengers lived near each other and intermarried in Plymouth and Cape Cod.

Surnames offer clues to identity using genealogy. Surnames came into existence about 1000 and the Norman Conquest. Most common were names derived from the name of a father or ancestor, typically by the addition of a prefix or suffix, "Son of John" became Johnson. A trade or a location became the signifier.

When studying Pilgrim genealogy, it becomes obvious that many Pilgrim names did not go back further than about 1550. One possibility is that they were Jews who fled Spain during the Inquisition in 1492. It is our contention that many Jews fleeing persecution settled around Europe and took on surnames that reflected either their trade or geography. To the outside world they identified as Christians but within their tight knit community they retained Jewish practices. Their faith was based on each individual's direct connection to God. This particular concept would become the source of division and conflict when King James mandated the preeminence of the Church of England.

Genealogy provides data including names, dates, geography and personal stories. This information is essential to understanding the roles people play throughout history. For example, not understanding the ten year separation from the Mayflower landing and that of the Winthrop Fleet obliterates the story of our first Thanksgiving.

Knowing Brewster's history through genealogy establishes the data as to the reason that he went on with the Mayflower when the Speedwell was aborted. Knowing Hopkins' history gives insight to the reason he directed the Mayflower Compact and how he managed to keep the group united.

Different paths lead to different insights. Recognizing the differences between our Pilgrims and Puritans is significant and often overlooked. Understanding of the Wampanoag's and their relationship with the Pilgrims is missing. The motivations that brought the Separatists and the Merchant adventures to the Mayflower voyage were completely different. Upon their arrival in Plymouth their common consideration was survival.

There are three significant historical events that together formed our Thanksgiving tradition. Each was a victory over a monumental challenge. Each was followed by a celebration. In some sense these celebrations were a collective exhale that an existential crisis had been averted. They were a spontaneous display and recognition that against long odds, victory and indeed survival had been achieved. The celebrations each held unity as the common theme and that better days lay ahead.

Arguably, a fourth significant historical event was the Election of 2020 wherein the Thanksgiving message by President-Elect Joe Biden shows the status of our country immediately after his election. It shows his plan to institute the first program to address Covid-19. It also shows our country before the Insurrection.

CHAPTER 1 | RELIGIOUS INTENSITY

The Religious Intensity of the Tudor Monarchs enry VI ruled from 1485 to 1509. Henry VII became king in 1509. Henry and his first wife, Catherine of Aragon had one child, Mary I. He and Elizabeth of York had four children: Arthur, who died young, Henry VIII, Margaret and Mary. In 1536 Henry VIII broke from the Catholic Church because the Pope would not give him an annulment from his first wife, so he could marry Anne Boleyn.

King Henry VIII established the Church of England with himself and all succeeding Monarchs as the head but maintaining the basic Catholic tenets. The Pope and all Catholic Clergy were removed and replaced by new Clergy respecting the monarchy. They have made changes to the liturgy over the years beginning with Thomas Cranmer under King Edward IV. In the American Revolution the Anglican Church was supplanted by the Episcopal Church. The teachings were the same, but the English hierarchy was eliminated and replaced by American clergy.

Henry VIII and Anne Boleyn had one child, who, ultimately, became Queen Elizabeth. He had one son, Edward VI, with his next wife, Jane Seymour. He had no children with his last three wives. Meanwhile, The Protestant Reformation, which began separately in Europe, was based on separation from the Catholic Church for different reasons. The Reformation is generally considered to have started with the publication of the Ninety-five Theses by Martin Luther in 1517.

Henry VIII died in 1547 and was succeeded by his son, Edward VI, who was nine at the time. Edward was sickly and died in 1553. Lady Jane Grey became Queen as manipulated by Edward VI and his advisors as a means to preserve Protestant rule. Her reign lasted nine days. Palace treachery was led by Mary. As the eldest daughter of Henry VIII, Mary had been passed over years prior in favor of the male heir, Edward. The turn of events was swift and Jane was beheaded.

Queen Mary I, reestablished the Catholic Church once again as the Church of State. It was a tumultuous and violent five years. Mary I, whose mother had been beheaded, held a grudge and became a rabid leader of England. Among other actions, she had Protestants burned at the stake. Bloody Mary.

The reign of Queen Mary I ended abruptly when Elizabeth had her beheaded. Queen Elizabeth I, the daughter of Henry VIII and Anne Boleyn, thus became Queen and reinstalled the Church of England. Her 44 year reign (the Elizabethan Age) ended the Tudor Dynasty that had begun with her grandfather, Henry VII. Known as the Virgin Queen, she produced no offspring. The Church of England was preeminent during her time on the throne.

The Church of England was totally disconnected from the Pope and the Catholic Church itself. It was founded on Catholic precepts directly. The Church of England, however, had nothing to do with the Protestant Reformation and the precepts of Luther, Calvin and the theologians who challenged the precepts of the Catholic Church.

In actuality, three separate and distinct religious streams were in effect.

- ➢ The Catholic Church
- ➢ The Church of England which was based on Catholic precepts with the King replacing the Pope as Supreme Head with English hierarchy.
- ➢ The Protestant Reformation, which challenged both the Catholic Church and Catholic Precepts. They did not have

an intermediary between individuals and God, whereas the Pope or the King was directly connected to God.

Historians have often overlooked the distinctions between these three groups. The Church of England is termed Protestant despite having no theology derived from the Reformation itself and the early leaders.

Elizabeth I did not have sufficient objection to the existence of The Church of Scotland to make a stance against it. There were no significant controversies regarding religion in England during her reign. It is said that many of her decisions were based on the cost of an issue to challenge. Protestant teachings were not her passion to fight. Notably, The Church of Scotland was not under her leadership.

Queen Elizabeth installed two primary acts: the Act of Supremacy, which rejected the Pope and established the Monarch as the Supreme Head of the Church, and the Act of Uniformity, which regulated the Book of Common Prayer and other practices. These acts were aimed at consolidating the power of the Church of England under her rule and to regulate the practice of primary tenets. (Encyclopedia Britannica)

Since the Reign of Edward IV and the religious leadership of Thomas Cranmer, the Church of England has had no further theological connection to the Catholic Church. The Anglican edicts and teachings have followed their singular stream in itself. Over time some Anglican precepts have crossed into mainstream Protestantism, so this line has blurred. Today, the Church of England and the Episcopal Church are considered Protestant. The extreme differences of the religions during this period and the foundational precepts are not recognized in our times. Where there were once distinct lines, there is now commonality.

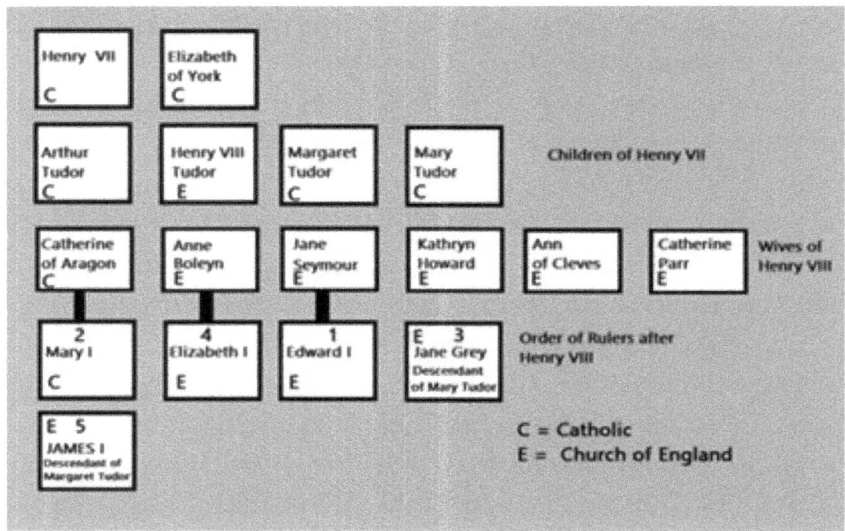

The Tudor Monarchs

Religious Controversies

The religious stability under Queen Elizabeth ended with her death in 1603.

A century earlier, Henry VIII's sister, Margaret, had married King James IV of Scotland. Her great-grandson eventually became King of Scotland as a baby. His upbringing was Protestant. Upon Queen Elizabeth's death in 1603 he became King James of Scotland and England establishing the House of Stuart in both thrones.

The foundations of the churches are significant in understanding the conflicts during this period.

The Catholic Church continues under the various Popes and basic theology.

The Protestant Reformation began in Wittenberg, Germany, on October 31, 1517, when Martin Luther, a teacher and a monk, published a document he called Disputation on the Power of Indulgences, or 95 Theses. The document was a series of 95 ideas about Christianity that he invited people to debate with him. These ideas were controversial because they directly contradicted the Catholic Church's teachings. (National Geographic Society)

Luther's statements challenged the Catholic Church's role as intermediary between people and God, specifically when it came to the indulgence system, which in part allowed people to purchase a certificate of pardon for the punishment of their sins. Luther argued against the practice of buying or earning forgiveness, believing instead that salvation is a gift God gives to those who have faith. (National Geographic Society)

The earliest Scottish reformers were under Lutheran influence but were subsequently influenced by the Swiss reformers. The Calvinistic tone of the Scottish Reformation was ascribable to John Knox, who became the leader of the Scottish Reformation. Knox's admiration for John Calvin and for the Reformation that Calvin led in Geneva is evident in Knox's Scots Confession, in the Book of Common Order (often known as Knox's liturgy), and in the Book of Discipline, the last of which discussed a plan for a godly church and commonwealth. The Scottish reformers held a parliament in August 1560, which abolished the authority of the pope in Scotland, adopted the Scots Confession, and forbade the celebration of mass. The Reformation established a third mainstream theology. (Church of Scotland)

The struggle was long and complicated, but, when William and Mary became the English monarchs in 1689, a century later, Presbyterianism was permanently established in Scotland by constitutional act. (Church of Scotland)

It wasn't until the two thrones were united that major conflicts arose. James chose to give the Church of England precedence. In 1604 he commissioned an English translation of the Christian Bible with instructions to adhere to Church of England precepts rather than those of the Reformation.

Concurrently, there were small groups of commoners who were separatists from the Church of England. Consider it a grass roots approach wherein small groups followed their personal religious views. They believed each person had a direct, intimate relationship with God. They were adherents of the Old Testament and were against the puritan ideas for reform. It was by no means an organized national movement. They were not connected to the Reformation itself.

> *Robert Browne was one of the active protesters. He was only active from 1579 to 1585 but his writings were quite influential. His most important works were published at Middelburg in 1582: A Treatise of Reformation without Tarying for Anie, in which he asserted the right of the church to effect necessary reforms without the authorisation of the civil magistrate; and A Booke which sheweth the life and manners of all True Christians, which set out the theory of Congregational independence. He then went back to being an Anglican Priest. (Robert Browne Brownist)*

Pastor John Robinson was leader of one of three groups who followed Browne's teachings. He joined the small independent group at Scrooby Manor. They called themselves Brownists and we know them today as pilgrims. His deacons were William Brewster and Thomas Blossom.

THE EFFECT OF THE SPANISH INQUISITION

The Day of Expulsion in 1492 from Spain was the day Columbus sailed with three ships to the New World. Most of his crew were Jews and most likely felt the risks of Columbus' expedition were preferable to certain death at the hands of Spanish authorities. There are countless unknown stories of survival along with the gruesome deaths of most.

There were many Jews who professed conversion in order to escape punishment, but continued to practice Jewish theology in secret. In England there was a path that was open particularly to the wealthy.

Some history is necessary. Around the year 1,000 there were two exceptional inventions: The steel rim to the wheel and the steel nose to the plow. For the first time in history farmers could produce far more than they could sell locally. Jews became the traders. They had the advantage of a common language that bridged borders. Then, because of their wealth, they became money lenders to the Royals. The Magna Carta has two sections that specify debts to the Jewish Traders.

Excerpts from the Magna Carta

* (10) If anyone who has borrowed a sum of money from Jews dies before the debt has been repaid, his heir shall pay no interest on the debt for so long as he remains under age, irrespective of whom he holds his lands. If such a debt falls into the hands of the Crown, it will take nothing except the principal sum specified in the bond.
* (11) If a man dies owing money to Jews, his wife may have her dower and pay nothing towards the debt from it. If he leaves children that are under age, their needs may also be provided for on a scale appropriate to the size of his holding of lands. The debt is to be paid out of the residue, reserving the service due to his feudal lords. Debts owed to persons other than Jews are to be dealt with similarly. (English translation of Magna Carta)

Anti-Semitism in England flared as King John and many in the aristocracy owed huge debts to the Jews. Jewish families were forced to leave England. Traders continued to market goods and, apparently, make loans.

Because of the Inquisition, Spanish Jews were forced to relocate. The centuries old network of Jewish traders had long established relationships with locals and leaders in the market towns. They aided discrete Jews with financial means to relocate to safe havens. The wealth of migrant Jews enabled them to purchase land and pay off those that may have otherwise objected. A low profile, assimilation and swearing allegiance to The Church of England was mandatory. In the privacy of their own homes they continued to practice Judaism. Secrecy was paramount. With successive generations, maintaining Jewish traditions was difficult.

KING JAMES I Reign

Protestantism in Scotland had been long established and unchallenged. It wasn't until the two thrones were united under King James that major conflicts arose. James chose to give the Church of England precedence. In 1604 he commissioned an English translation of the Christian Bible with instructions to adhere to Church of England precepts.

The King James Version of the Bible was published in 1611. A clash of religious ideology ensued. The focus shifted to the New Testament.

The Five Articles of Perth give a clear statement of the main points of contention. They were introduced by King James in 1618 to impose practices on the Church of Scotland in an attempt to integrate it with those of the Church of England. These were the predominant issues during his reign. The articles required:

> ➢ kneeling during communion
> ➢ elimination of private baptism
> ➢ elimination of private communion for the sick or infirm
> ➢ confirmation by a bishop
> ➢ the observance of "Holy Days" including Christmas and Easter

These articles were aligned with the Church of England. Article 5 requiring observance of Christmas and Easter caused the most serious outrage. These Separatists were dedicated to the "Old Testament" as termed by King James.

PERTH
ASSEMBLY

CONTAINING

1 The Proceedings thereof.
2 The Proofe of the Nullitie thereof.
2 Reasons presented thereto against the recei-
   ving the fiue new *Articles* imposed.
4 The oppositenesse of it to the proceedings and
   oath of the whole state of the Land. *An.*1581.
5 Proofes of the unlawfulnesse of the said fiue
   Articles, *viz.* 1. Kneeling in the act of Re-
   ceiving the Lords Supper. 2. Holy daies.
   3. Bishopping. 4. Private Baptisme. 5. Private Communion.

EXOD. 20. 7.

*Thou shalt not take the name of the Lord thy God in vaine, for the
Lord will not hold him guiltlesse that takith his name in vaine.*

COLOS. 2. 8.

*Beware left there be any that spoyle you through Philosophy & vain de-
ceit, through the traditions of men, according to the rudiments of the
World, and not of Christ.*

MDCXIX.

William Brewster was a printer by trade and a Deacon of the Brownist congregation. From the onset, he was vocal activist against

King James' religious principles. In 1611, Pastor John Robinson, Deacons Brewster and Thomas Blossom and many of the Brownist congregation relocated to Leiden, Holland. In 1618, Brewster published this flyer in response to the 5 Articles of Perth. He immediately became the target for authorities opposing his activism.

> "The Secession historian Thomas M'Crie tries to hint at the leading objections against them. Others like Robert Baillie accepted the liturgical changes even elaborating an exhaustive defense of kneeling at communion in protracted correspondence with David Dickson, the minister for the parish of Irvine. The articles were reluctantly accepted by the General Assembly of the Church at Perth in 1618, and were not ratified by the Scottish Parliament until July 1621; it was known by some as Black Saturday and was accompanied by a thunderstorm. The approving Act was repealed by the Confession of Faith Ratification Act of 1690. In 1619 the Pilgrims who were in exile in Leiden published a critical tract about the Five Articles, entitled the Perth Assembly, which nearly led to William Brewster's arrest. "(Five Articles of Perth)

The objections to the Articles of Perth indicate a clear possibility to the legends that our Pilgrims had been Jews who fled Spain in the Inquisition. There may have been many families who fled with the intention to keep Jewish precepts in private, while not having a public identity.

> "The reason the Jews came to the New World should be evident — they were fleeing the Inquisition. The first to come and live came as Marranos, a somewhat derogatory term for a converted Jew. (Many Jews became nominal converts to Christianity in order to escape persecution or death, but they retained their faith privately and remained Jewish in their hearts.) But even the converts often had difficulty finding acceptance aboard vessels sailing west. For this reason many tried to destroy every scrap of evidence that might show that they were or ever had been Jewish." (Craton, John)

When Pastor John Robinson moved to Leiden, he and several hundred followers determined their best opportunity for their congregation was to settle in a place where they would be left alone. Without understanding their history, the times they were living and their singular identity, it is not possible to comprehend the unity of minds, their souls, their identity and their experiences. They were outsiders. Governor William Bradford gave account of William Brewster's influence on the Separatist movement from its early beginnings:

> *"In 1608, after the agreement to separate from the church of England, the Separatists of the Scrooby congregation covenanted together to form a church: They shook off the yoke of antichristian bondage, and as ye Lord's free people, joyned themselves (by a covenant of the Lord) into a church estate, in ye fellowship of ye Gospel, to walke in all his wayes, made known or to be made known unto them, according to their best endeavours, whatsoever it should cost them, the Lord assisting them. On December 15, 1617, William Brewster and the congregation's pastor, John Robinson, wrote a letter from Leyden, Holland, to Sir Edwin Sandys, a London financier, in which they explained the Separatists' situation and plans: Knit together as a body in most strict and sacred bond and covenant of the lord, of the violation whereof we make great conscience, and by virtue whereof we so hold ourselves straitly tied to all care of each other's good, and of the whole by everyone and so mutually. (Bradford)*

In Holland, Pastor John Robinson and his followers faced a different type of challenge. Whereas England tried to impose conformity, Holland was at the forefront of The Enlightenment. Baruch Spinoza, a Jew, was leading the Enlightenment Movement. New ideas and questions were open to debate. This was yet another fervent challenge to the Brownists private community. They had traditional precepts, but after more than a century, they had had their own, quite separate, spiritual identity. They had fears that their own children would take on the radicalism of The Enlightenment. The focus on the Old Testament is the significant indicator. Moses and the Jews fled from the persecution in Egypt in search of the Promised Land. A similar call to migrate to the New World became practical and symbolic.

In 1629, when a church was founded at Salem in the Massachusetts Bay Colony, William Brewster made this comment:

> *The church that had been brought over the ocean now saw another church, the first-born in America, holding the same faith in the same simplicity of self-government under Christ alone. (Bradford)*

One could argue that the Pilgrims had indeed found their promised land.

CHAPTER 2 | VANTAGE POINT FROM STEPHEN HOPKINS

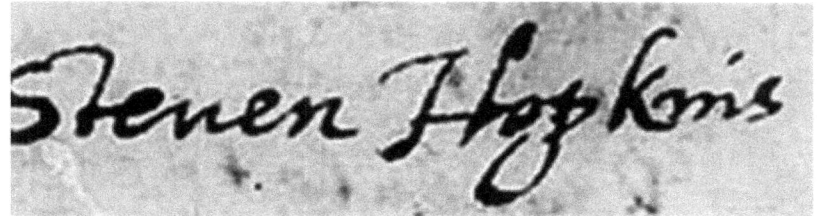

A Mayflower passenger, Mr. Stephen Hopkins was a Gentleman and a Stranger. On this voyage, Pilgrims referred to themselves as Saints and all others as Strangers. They were also classified as Separatists or Non-Separatists from the Church of England. He probably had the most wealth and the most education.

In 1609, Stephen Hopkins left his wife and three children in Hampshire, while he pursued adventure and fortune on an armada destined for Jamestown. His Jamestown adventure was literally the story for legends. Shakespeare wrote "The Tempest" with his character as Stephano. It was based on the crossing of the Sea Venture, wherein Hopkins was clerk to the chaplain, The Reverend Richard Buck.

In May 1609, James I issued the second charter to the Virginia Company. Sir Thomas Smith (Smythe) was appointed Treasurer of the Virginia Company. On June 2, not long after her launch, the

Virginia Company's ship "Sea Venture" sailed on its maiden voyage from Plymouth, England, bound for Jamestown, Virginia. She was newly built in 1609 in Aldeburgh, Suffolk, England, and was England's first purpose-designed emigrant ship. She displaced 300 tons, cost £1,500, and differed from her contemporaries primarily in her internal arrangements. Her guns were placed on her main deck, rather than below decks as was then the norm. This meant the ship did not need double-timbering, and she may have been the first single-timbered, armed merchant ship built in England. Her hold was sheathed and furnished for passengers. She was armed with eight nine-pounder demi-culverins, eight five-pounder sakers (cannon), four three-pounder falcons (also cannon), and four arquebuses. Her uncompleted journey to Jamestown appears to have been her maiden voyage. Admiral Somers was on overall command of the "Third Supply Relief Fleet" of nine vessels. The newly appointed then-deputy Governor-elect of Virginia, Sir Thomas Gates, was the most senior passenger in order of precedence.

Captain Christopher Newport was chief officer of the fleet. George Yeardley was the commander of land forces under Gates. 600 colonists included John Rolfe and his pregnant first wife, who died later in Bermuda. The fleet was to relieve the struggling British colony established in 1607 under Captain John Smith after the failure of the Roanoke Island venture of Sir Walter Raleigh. It was then the largest and most expensive colonization ever undertaken by Britain. (Forbes, K)

Stephen Hopkins was the clerk for Reverend Richard Buck, the Anglican chaplain of the Virginia settlement. Hopkins had a good education and had served as the assistant clergy at Church of St. Mary the Virgin in Wotton-under-edge in Gloucestershire, England. The clerk for a minister would have been required to be literate in both Latin and in English. The clerk would read the portion of an epistle for the service and to sing from the Psalter and Book of Common Prayer.

Thus, Hopkins would have been well qualified to serve as the Clerk for Reverend Buck and the fleet.

A 'most dreadfull Tempest'

The Sea Venture sailed into history and into literature as it was shipwrecked in Bermuda. A storm raged for five days and the ship went aground just offshore.

There were 150 passengers, who went ashore and set up living accommodations. An Anglican service of Evensong was said that first evening.

William Strachey was a member of the Virginia Company chartered by King James I to establish a colony in North America. He was a passenger on the Sea Venture as well as a chronicler and author. Regarding the shipwreck, he wrote,

> "On St. James Day, being Monday, the clouds gathering thick upon us and the wind singing and whistling most unusually, a dreadful storm began to blow from out the northeast, which, swelling and roaring as it were by fits, at length did beat all night from Heaven; which like a hell of darkness, turned black upon us . . . For four-and-twenty hours the storm in a restless tumult had blown so exceedingly as we could not apprehend in our imaginations any possibility of greater violence; yet did we still find it not only more terrible but more constant, fury added to fury, and one storm urging a second more outrageous than the former . . . It could not be said to rain. The waters like whole rivers did flood in the air. Winds and seas were as mad as fury and rage could make them. Howbeit this was not all. It pleased God to bring greater affliction yet upon us; for in the beginning of the storm we had received likewise a mighty leak...._

All the passengers were able to make it to the island since the wreck occurred on a reef close to the shore. Ultimately, the group built two small ships to proceed to Jamestown. However, Hopkins and others wanted to stay in Bermuda. He wrote:

"[there] were two apparent reasons to stay them even in this place; first, abundance of God's providence of all manner of good foode; next, some hope in reasonable time, when they might grow weary of the place, to build a small Barke, with the skill and help of the aforesaid Nicholas Bennit, whom they insinuated to them to be of the conspiracy, that so might get cleere from hence at their own pleasures . . .

It was Hopkins' contention that the Virginia Charter did not come into effect until they reached Virginia. Hopkins advocated that the shipwreck survivors should remain in Bermuda and create a new charter. This action was considered mutinous by the leadership group, He was found guilty of mutiny and sentenced to hang.

From Strachey's record of the voyage. "But so penitent hee was and made so much moane, alleadging the mine of his Wife and Children in this his trespass,".

Hopkins pleaded that his execution would cause the ruin of his wife and family back in London. There were strong pleas for mercy. The ship's captain, Christopher Newport, requested that the Governor release him. Stephen Hopkins was pardoned. (Pertz, B)

The two newly built vessels, the Patience and the Deliverance, arrived at Jamestown on 24 May 1610. As this story spread, it inspired Shakespeare for his play "The Tempest". It was written and first performed on 11/1/1611. The Tempest explores the consequences of European settlement in the New World. The theme is that the powerful must show mercy.

"O wonder! How many goodly creatures are there here! How beauteous mankind is! O brave new world That has such people in 't! (The Tempest, Shakespeare)

Upon reaching Jamestown, Hopkins had considerable interactions with the natives. Jamestown was a colony dedicated to financial gain. While profit was Hopkins' motive, as was most others, he left after four years without success.

Back in Hampshire, his wife, Mary, had died, leaving Hopkins to be sole charge of his children. A few years later he married Elizabeth and had another child.

He was recruited to join the Mayflower passengers, since he had experience communicating with the natives.

The Mayflower leaders, their families and servants were devout Separatists. There were also a few servants on the way to employment in Jamestown. Hopkins was a Non-Separatist, who was seeking financial benefits. Quite possibly, he had no idea of the religious fervour of the congregation, when he joined the expedition.

CHAPTER 3 |
THE MAYFLOWER VOYAGE

S peedwell, and sailed to Southampton, England to meet the the Pilgrims left Leiden, Holland in their newly chartered boat, the Mayflower, which had been chartered by their English investors. The Mayflower was an old cargo ship that had been primarily used for transporting wine from Bordeaux to England. It was nearing the end of its commercial viability and in fact was scrapped in 1624. The Speedwell leaked so badly they had to stop at both Dartmouth and Plymouth in Cornwall. The Speedwell was ultimately abandoned in Plymouth, England.

Several factors influenced who would be chosen for the trimmed down group of passengers for the only seaworthy vessel. The revised passenger list for the Mayflower to "New Israel" were fairly evenly split between Separatists and Non-Separatists. It is likely that funding by the Non-Separatists was critical to keeping the voyage moving forward. They were also known as the "merchant adventurers" who were making the trip for financial gain. Thomas Westin was an agent who recruited these types of adventurous passengers, including Steven Hopkins.

Pastor John Robinson's two deacons were on the Speedwell as the religious leaders of the Separatists. William Brewster was transferred to The Mayflower. His inflammatory writing on the Articles of Perth made him a target of the Church of England. Going against the church was particularly dangerous under King James. Choosing Brewster for the voyage was imperative as a mater of safety and probably survival.

Deacon Blossom returned to Leiden to assist Robinson and organize the next three ships. He became the leader of the flock, when Pastor Robinson died in 1626. In 1629 he joined the Pilgrims in

Plymouth with six ships. Thus, the entire community relocated to Plymouth.

On the Mayflower, there were 102 passengers, and 30 crew members as well as pigs, goats, chickens and two dogs. They spent a month on board in port getting supplies and approvals, before embarking. They spent two months at sea from September 9 to November 11. In October the storms began raging. It was a tumultuous and terrifying time. Including the trip from Leiden they had been below deck for four months. They were seasick during much of their two months at sea.

The firsthand account of Ship's Log describes the intensity of the voyage.

THE SHIP'S LOG

SUNDAY, Sept. 10/Sept. 20 Comes in with wind E.N.E. Gale holds. Distance lost, when ship bore up for Plymouth, more than regained.

MONDAY, Sept. 11/Sept. 21 Same; and so without material change, the daily record of wind, weather, and the ship's general course--the repetition of which would be both useless and wearisome-- continued through the month and until the vessel was near half the seas over. Fine warm weather and the "harvestmoon." The usual equinoctial weather deferred.

SATURDAY, Sept. 23/Oct. 3 One of the seamen, some time sick with a grievous disease, died in a desperate manner. The first death and burial at sea of the voyage.

A sharp change. Equinoctial weather, followed by stormy westerly gales; encountered cross winds and continued fierce storms. Ship shrewdly shaken and her upper works made very leaky. One of the main beams in the midships was bowed and cracked. Some fear that the ship could not be able to perform the voyage. The chief of the company perceiving the mariners to fear the sufficiency of the ship (as appeared by their mutterings) they entered into serious consultation with the Master and other officers of the ship, to consider, in time, of the danger, and rather to return than to cast themselves into a desperate and inevitable peril.

There was great distraction and difference of opinion amongst the mariners themselves. Fain would they do what would be done for their wages' sake, being now near half the seas over; on the other hand, they were loath to hazard their lives too desperately. In examining of all opinions, the Master and others affirmed they knew the ship to be strong and firm under water, and for the buckling bending or bowing of the main beam, there was a great iron scrue the passengers brought out of Holland which would raise the beam into its place. The which being done, the carpenter and Master affirmed that a post put under it, set firm in the lower deck, and otherwise bound, would make it sufficient. As for the decks and upper works, they would caulk them as well as they could; and though with the working of the ship they would not long keep staunch, yet there would otherwise be no great danger if they did not over press her with sails. So they resolved to proceed.

In sundry of these stormes, the winds were so fierce and the seas so high, as the ship could not bear a knot of sail, but was forced to hull drift under bare poles for divers days together. A succession of strong westerly gales. In one of the heaviest storms, while lying at hull, [hove to D.W.] a lusty young man, one of the passengers, John Howland by name, coming upon some occasion above the gratings latticed covers to the hatches, was with the seel [roll] of the ship thrown into the sea, but caught hold of the topsail halliards, which hung overboard and ran out at length; yet he held his hold, though he was sundry fathoms under water, till he was hauled up by the same rope to the brim of the water, and then with a boat hook and other means got into the ship again and his life saved. He was something ill with it.

The equinoctial disturbances over and the strong October gales, the milder, warmer weather of late October followed.

Mistress Elizabeth Hopkins, wife of Master Stephen Hopkins, of Billericay, in Essex, was delivered of a son, who, on account of the circumstances of his birth, was named Oceanus, the first birth aboard the ship during the voyage.

A succession of fine days, with favoring winds.

MONDAY Nov. 6/16 William Butten; a youth, servant to Doctor Samuel Fuller, died. The first of the passengers to die on this voyage.

MONDAY Nov. 7/17 The body of William Butten committed to the deep. The first burial at sea of a passenger, on this voyage. MONDAY Nov. 8/18 Signs of land.(SHIP'S LOG)

The tenor of this log provides an extraordinary reference point for understanding the journey and the onset into the first year of the Mayflower Colony.

One of the servants, John Howland, went above and was swept overboard. He was saved because he caught a rope hanging over the side of the ship. It is easy to classify his being saved as a miracle. The odds were certainly not in his favor. His story is particularly fascinating. After arrival, he led an active, contributory life and was the longest living passenger. He convinced two of his brothers to immigrate. His descendants include FDR, Bush '41, Barbara Bush, and, obviously, Bush '43.

List of Mayflower Passengers

Note: An asterisk on a name indicates those who died in the winter of 1620–21

Members of the Leiden, Holland Congregation.

Isaac Allerton (possibly Suffolk), Mary (Norris) Allerton*, wife (Berkshire)

Bartholomew Allerton, 7, son (Leiden) Remember Allerton, 5, daughter (Leiden). Mary Allerton, 3, daughter (Leiden).

Bradford, William (Austerfield, Yorkshire) Dorothy (May) Bradford*, wife (Isle of Ely, Cambershire)

William Brewster (possibly Nottingham). Mary Brewster, wife. Fear Brewster, later married Isaac Allerton Love/True Love Brewster, 9, son (Leiden). Wrestling Brewster, 6, son (Leiden).

Carver, John* (possibly Yorkshire). Katherine (Leggett) (White) Carver*, wife (prob, Sturton-le-Steeple, Nottinghamshire)

Chilton, James* (Canterbury, Kent). Mrs. (James) Chilton*, wife. Mary Chilton, 13, daughter (Sandwich, Kent).

Cooke, Francis John Cooke, 13, son (Leiden). Cooper, Humility, 1, (probably Leiden) baby daughter of Robert Cooper, in company of her aunt Ann Cooper Tilley, wife of Edward Tiley Crackstone/ Crackon, John* (possibly Colchester, Essex). John Crackstone, son.

Fletcher, Moses* (Sandwich, Jent).

Fuller, Edward* (Redenhall, Norfolk). Mrs. (Edward) Fuller*, wife. Samuel Fuller, 12, son.

Fuller, Samuel (Redenhall, Norfolk), (brother to Edward).

Goodman, John (possibly Northampton).

Priest, Degory*

Rogers, Thomas* (Watford, Northampton.)

Joseph Rogers, 17, son (Watford, Northamptonshire).

Samson, Henry, 16, (Henlow, Bedfordshire) child in company of his uncle and aunt Edward and Ann Tilley.

Tilley, Edward* (Henlow, Bedfordshire)

Ann (Cooper) Tilley* (Henlow, Bedfordshire) wife of Edward and aunt of Humility Cooper and Henry Samson.

Tilley, John* (Henlow, Bedfordshire).

Joan (Hurst) (Rogers) Tilley*, wife (Henlow, Bedfordshire). Elizabeth Tilley, 13, daughter (Henlow, Bedfordshire).

Tinker, Thomas* (possibly Norfolk). Mrs. Thomas Tinker*, wife. boy Tinker*, son, died in the winter of 1620.

Turner, John* (possibly Norfolk). boy Turner*, son, died in the winter of 1620. boy Turner*, younger son. died in the winter of 1620.

White, William* William White's sister Bridget was John Robinson's wife. John Robinson was Pastor of the Pilgrim Fathers leading the Separatists since his days at college at Cambridge

Susanna White, wife, widowed February 21, 1621. She subsequently married Pilgrim Edward Winslow

Resolved White, 5, son, wife was Judith Vassal.

Peregrine White, son. Born on board the Mayflower in Cape Cod Harbor in late November 1620. First European born to the Pilgrims in America.

Williams, Thomas

Winslow, Edward (Droit. Worcestershire). Elizabeth (Barker) Winslow, wife

Servants to Leiden Group

Butten, William* (possibly Nottingham), "a youth", indentured servant of Samuel Fuller, died during the voyage. He was the first passenger to die on November 16, three days before Cape Cod was sighted.

Dorothy, teenager, maidservant of John Carver.

Hooke, John*, (probably Norwich, Norfolk) age 13, apprenticed to Isaac Allerton, died during the first winter.

Howland, John, (Fenstanton, Huntingdonshire), about 21, manservant and executive assistant for Governor John Carver.

Latham, William, (possibly Lancashire), age 11, servant and apprentice to the John Carver family. His parents died in Leiden Minter, Desire, (Norwich, Norfolk), a servant of John Carver whose parents died in Leiden.

More, Ellen (Elinor)*, (Shipton, Shropshire), age 8, assigned as a servant of Edward Winslow. She died from illness sometime in November 1620 soon after the arrival of Mayflower in Cape Cod harbor and likely was buried ashore there in an unmarked grave it was originally placed sometime in the mid-1690s. More, Mary*, (Shipton, Shropshire) age 4, assigned as a servant of William Brewster. She died sometime in the winter of 1620/1621. She and her sister Ellen are recognized on the Pilgrim Memorial Tomb in Plymouth.

More, Jasper*, (Shipton, Shropshire), age 7, indentured to John Carver. He died from illness on board Mayflower on December 6, 1620 and likely was buried ashore on Cape Cod in an unmarked grave.

More, Richard (Shipton, Shropshire), age 6, indentured to William Brewster. He is buried in the Charter Street Burial Ground in Salem, Massachusetts. He is the only Mayflower passenger to have his gravestone still where it was originally placed sometime in the mid1690s. Also buried nearby in the same cemetery were his wives Christian Hunter More and Jane (Crumpton) More

Passengers recruited by Thomas Weston, of London

Merchant Adventurers

Billington, John (possibly Lancashire) Eleanor Billington, wife.
John Billington, 16, son.
Francis Billington, 14, son.
    Britteridge, Richard* (possibly Sussex).[31]
    Browne, Peter (Dorking, Surrey).
    Clarke, Richard*
    Eaton, Francis (Bristol,Gloucestershire)
    Sarah Eaton*, wife.
    Samuel Eaton, 1, son.
    Gardiner, Richard (Harwich, Essex).
    Hopkins, Stephen (Upper Clatford, Hampshire).
    Elizabeth (Fisher) Hopkins, wife.
    Giles Hopkins, 12, son by first marriage
    Constance Hopkins, 14, daughter by first marriage (Hursley, Hampshire).
    Damaris Hopkins, 1–2, daughter. (She died soon in Plymouth Colony and her parents later had another daughter with the same name.)
    Oceanus Hopkins,born on board the *Mayflower* while en route to the New World.
    Margesson, Edmund* (possibly Norfolk)
    Martin, Christopher* 38 (Great Burstead, Essex). Mayflower Governor & Purchasing Agent.
    Mary (Prowe) Martin*, wife.
    Mullins, William* (Dorking, Surrey).
    Alice Mullins*, wife.
    Priscilla Mullins, 18, daughter.
    Joseph Mullins*, 14, son.
    Prowe, Solomon* (Billericay, Essex). Son of Mary Prowe
    Rigsdale, John* (possibly Lincolnshire).[34] Alice Rigsdale*, wife.
    Standish, Myles (Standish, Wigan, Lancashire). Military Expert for Colony.
    Rose Standish*, wife.

Warren, Richard (Hertford, England).

Winslow, Gilbert (Droitwich, Worcestershire), brother to Pilgrim Edward Winslow but not known to have lived in Leiden.

Servants of Merchant Adventurers

Carter, Robert*, (possibly Surrey), teenager, servant or apprentice to William Mullins, shoemaker.

Doty, Edward, (possibly Lincolnshire) age probably about 21, servant to Stephen Hopkins.

Holbeck, William*, age likely under 21, servant to William White.

Langemore, John*, age under 21, servant to Christopher Martin

Leister, Edward also spelled Leitster, (possibly vicinity of London), aged over 21, servant to Stephen Hopkins.

Thompson (or Thomson), Edward*, age under 21, in the care of the William White family, first passenger to die after the *Mayflower* reached Cape Cod. (Hampshire).

CHAPTER 4 | MAYFLOWER COMPACT

Finally, on 11/11/1620 the Mayflower was ready to touch land. BUT! It was far north of their intended destination in Virginia. The Charter was no longer valid in this location. Hopkins lived through a similar experience when he landed in Bermuda. He most certainly would have been alarmed at having this passionate religious group establish their own charter.

For Stephen Hopkins!
It was Raging Storms Again!

He was privately making plans for days, if not weeks as the destination changed. Doubtless, he planned every detail and every aspect. It was carefully, deliberately, intelligently conceived and rehearsed. He was totally focused.

His experience on The Sea Venture ten years prior gave him the knowledge that this was a CRITICAL situation. He took charge before there were any actions, before the others gave procedures a thought. The magnitude of making rules for governance must be the first order. It must be done on board. It must include every man. He was aware and prepared. He even had his biblical quotations. He was persuasive.

The leaders would have been irritated to no end at Hopkins demands for a new Charter. Everyone would have wanted to disembark immediately. Yet, Hopkins was adamant in his insistence that a new, legal document was mandatory before setting foot on land. He got his way. Every single adult male signed the Mayflower Compact. Not one was excluded because of status, money, titles, property, or religion. Hopkins managed the entire process of signing.

Protocol of times would have the men sign such a document in order of status. The order of the signatories is significant and shows deft management. Stephen Hopkins was a Cambridge graduate, had two servants and was the wealthiest if not the wealthiest person on the voyage. He took care to manipulate the order of the signatories as a means to create unity. The leaders of the new settlement were chosen to be the first signers. The next group to sign were the gentry. The order deliberately alternated between Separatists and adventurers giving each equal importance. Hopkins took care to have his signature be at the bottom of the ranked members. Commoners were next to sign followed by the servants with Hopkins' servants at the very bottom of the list. There was no argument, no rancor. No one would complain given each of them had precedent over him. Hopkins had carefully and successfully dedicated himself to inclusion without hierarchy.

In all probability, the egalitarian nature of the contract and the signatories was unprecedented.

The signing of the Mayflower Compact was the seminal moment at the very onset of our nation. It established a democratic tradition in the New World in which every man was included in the 'body politic' promising to obey 'just and equal laws'. The reality and the significance are regularly overlooked.

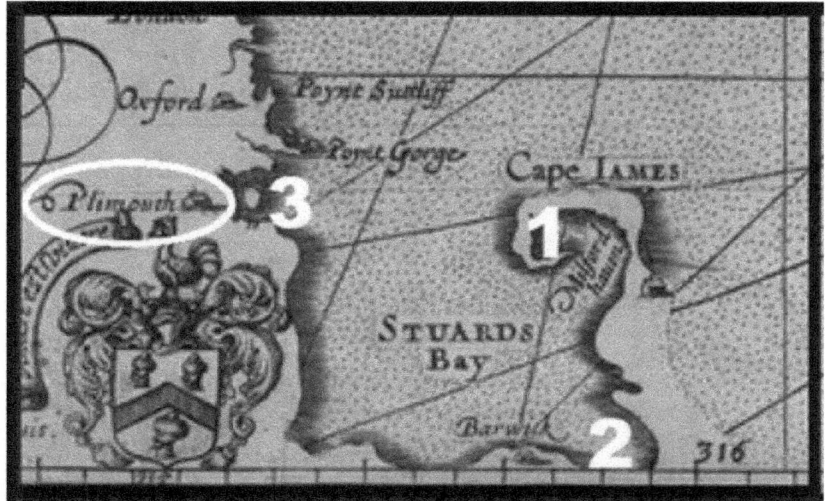

This is a section of Captain John Smith's 1616
Map. This was the map in their possession.

1 - The First Landing of the Mayflower was in Provincetown Harbor on Cape Cod. The Mayflower Compact was drafted and signed in the harbor before they disembarked. The Pilgrims then explored the Upper and Outer Cape.

2 -The First Encounter with Nauset, the People of the First Light right at the bend in the Bay.

3- The Plymouth Landing was made after they made their initial scouting trips and were more interested in crops than in fishing. Before they touched land the Mayflower Compact was agreed upon and signed.

Circled is the name Smith Designated on his 1616 Map.

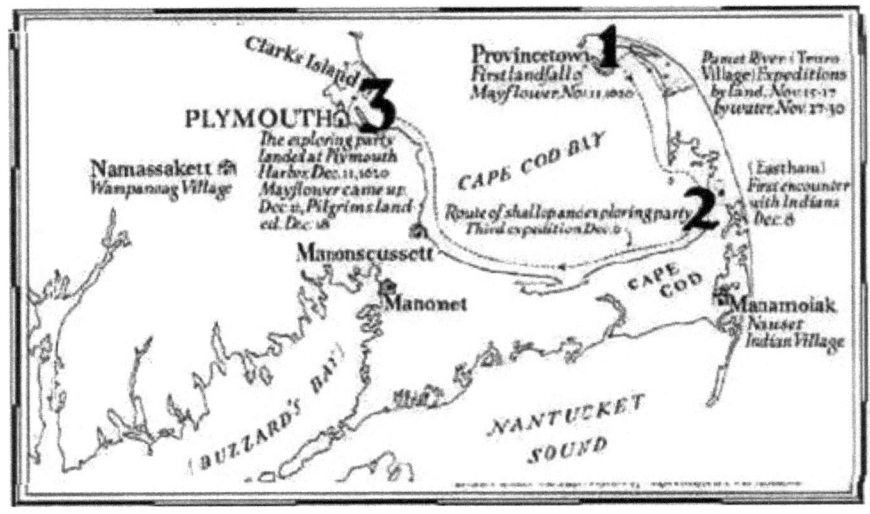

*Section of the Plymouth Plantation Map used to highlight
the Landing, First Encounter and Plymouth*

"The Mayflower Compact"

IN THE NAME OF GOD, AMEN. We, whose names are underwritten, the Loyal Subjects of our dread Sovereign Lord King James, by the Grace of God, of Great Britain, France, and Ireland, King, Defender of the Faith, &c. Having undertaken for the Glory of God, and Advancement of the Christian Faith, and the Honour of our King and Country, a Voyage to plant the first Colony in the northern Parts of Virginia;

(We) Do by these Presents, solemnly and mutually, in the Presence of God and one another, covenant and combine ourselves together into a civil Body Politick, for our better Ordering and Preservation, and Furtherance of the Ends aforesaid: And by Virtue Rewards hereof do enact, constitute, and frame, such just and equal Laws, Ordinances, Acts, Constitutions, and Officers, from time to time, as shall be thought most meet and convenient for the general Good of the Colony; unto which we promise all due Submission and Obedience.

IN WITNESS whereof we have hereunto subscribed our names at Cape-Cod the eleventh of November, in the Reign of our Sovereign

Lord King James, of England, France, and Ireland, the eighteenth, and of Scotland the fifty-fourth, Anno Domini; 1620."

How many of us have actually read The Mayflower Compact? It is generally not even included in the important documents in US history. Yet it set the ground rules for governance.

The outstanding feature is that the compact begins with the "NAME OF GOD," but It does not refer to a religion. There are no directives as to worship or religious behavior. The Compact is concerned solely with the governance of all the people. The document codifies the separation of church and state.

It set the precedent that every adult male would have equality under the law. Eighty-six words defined this Covenant, The Mayflower Compact. This should be understood and recognized as the preeminent founding document. This was the first covenant in America. It set the foundation for our moral and legal principles.

It should be noted that in this day the boundaries of "Virginia" were not well defined. It referred to much of the continent, excluding Spanish claims to the south.

THE SIGNATORS

SIGNATORIES OF THE MAYFLOWER COMPACT		
s Mr. John Carver	s Edward Tilley	s Degory Priest
s William Bradford	s John Tilley	s Thomas Williams
s Mr. Edward Winslow	MA Francis Cooke	s Gilbert Winslow
s Mr. William Brewster	MA Thomas Rogers	MA Edmund Margeson
s Mr. Isaac Allerton	s Thomas Tinker	MA Peter Browne
MA Capt. Myles Standish	MA John Rigsdale	MA Richard Britteridge
CREW John Alden	s Edward Fuller	s George Soule servant
s Mr. Samuel Fuller	s John Turner	MA Richard Clark
MA Mr. Christopher Martin	MA Francis Eaton	MA Richard Gardiner
MA Mr. William Mullens	s James Chilton	CREW John Allerton
S Mr. William White	s John Crackston	CREW Thomas English
MA Mr. Richard Warren	MA John Billingron	MA Edward Doty servant
s John Howland	s Moses Fletcher	MA Edward Leister servant
MA Mr. Stephen Hopkins	s John Goodman	

IN WITNESS whereof we have hereunto subscribed our names at

Cape-Cod the eleventh of November 1620

First Column Order

S Mr. John Carver Governor.

S Mr. William Bradford 2nd Governor

S Mr. Edward Winslow 3rd Governor

S Mr. William Brewster Religious Leader

S Mr. Isaac Allerton Financial Leader MA Capt. Myles Standish Military Leader

S Dr. Samuel Fuller

MA Mr. Christopher Martin MA Mr. William Mullens

S Mr. William White

MA Mr. Richard Warren

S John Howland Servant to Carver

MA Mr. Stephen Hopkins Indian Scout

THE SECOND AND THIRD COLUMNS

Commoners and servants filled both columns

The last men on the third column were S Gilbert Winslow Younger brother to Mr. Edward Winslow
S George Soule Indentured servant S John Allerton Younger brother to . Mr. Isaac Allerton

Followed by Two crew members
LASTLY MA Edward Doty Servant to Hopkins
MA Edward Leister Servant to Hopkins

This list shows exactly the problem Hopkins feared and resolved. His similar experience with the Sea Venture that nearly got him hanged proved invaluable. The ship was far afield from the original colony of Virginia. Thus, their charter was invalid. The problem was more alarming since the members of the Church in Leiden could make the rules favoring their religion. Hopkins got out ahead of this problem without drawing attention to his concerns. He pushed for a document that was inclusive of all men. It established a separation of church and state. There is a religious context, that was almost inescapable for the day, but there was no mention of specific religious practices. The Mayflower Compact reflected the belief of the Pilgrims that reach person had a direct connection to god. The religious conflicts in Europe carried forth to America.

The Mayflower Compact served to unite the group. The elected officials were placed before the religious leader and the wealthiest. No preference was given to Separatists and Non-Separatists (also referred to as Saints and Strangers). The challenges of the voyage made it clear that their success and survival depended on the unity and co-operation. As soon as they signed and disembarked, they were "A PEOPLE."

The Pilgrims would have landed in Virginia at the harvest season. One can only surmise why the Pilgrims undertook their venture against that daunting reality. They arrived far north of Virginia near the end of the Great Ice Age. There was no celebration or celebrating. They lost half of their members through scurvy and disease as a result of the festering conditions inside the boat, starvation and more.

CHAPTER 5 | THE WAMPANOAG

In Native American society, there are Nations or Confederations, such as the Wampanoag's and the Iroquois. Each Confederation is comprised of individual Tribes. The above map shows the Wampanoag Confederation or People, whereas the map below shows the Wampanoag Tribes on Cape Cod as they were in 1620.

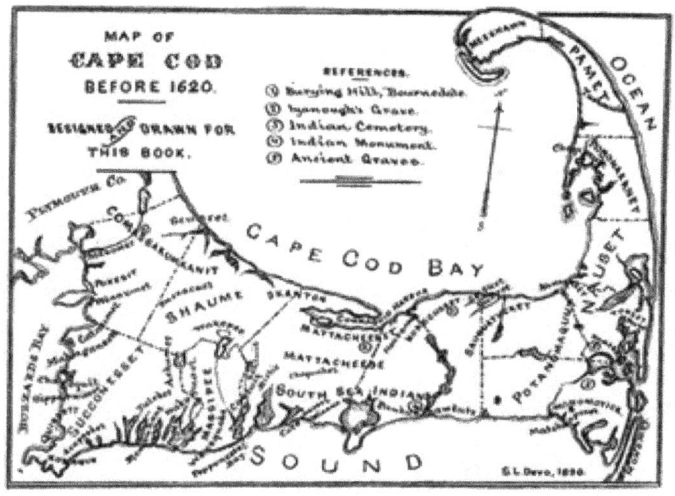

The Wampanoag People had existed for more than 12,000 years. However, beginning with the reign of Queen Elizabeth I, fishermen and traders began to appear in the New England area. The Wampanoag's were considered a great nation in the East of what is now Massachusetts. There were numerous subtribes. The Nauseas and Patuxent's had the first contact with the Pilgrims.

> *In 1600 the Wampanoag population was estimated at 12,000 with 40 villages divided roughly between 8,000 on the mainland and another 4,000 on the off-shore islands of Martha's Vineyard and Nantucket. There were three epidemics which swept across New England and the Canadian Maritimes between 1614 and 1620 that were especially devastating to the Wampanoag and neighboring tribes with mortality in many mainland villages (i.e. Patuxent) reaching 100%. When the Pilgrims landed in 1620, fewer than 2,000 mainland Wampanoag had survived. (*Saltzman*. Lee)*

Another source estimates a Wampanoag nation of 45,000, of which two-thirds of the entire, had perished because of illness. (Dina Gilio-Whitaker)

Tuberculosis and small pox were introduced via cargo ships, pirates and all manner of traders and explorers. The records of these ships are largely undocumented. There were no manifests until passengers started arriving in 1620. The epidemics with mass casualties were all prior the Mayflower landing. The context that is often overlooked is that the Pilgrims were arriving to an area whose population had been devastated.

CHAPTER 6 | EARLY EXPLORATIONS

S panish explorations starting with Columbus concentrated on the Caribbean, the southern coast of North America, and soon thereafter Central and South America.

A new focus began with Jacques Cartier in 1534. Francis I of France sent him to explore the New Lands. Cartier's mission was to find the fabled gold, jewels and all manner of riches that were certain to be awaiting him.

It appears that this action divided explorations of Spain to the South and France to the North of what is now Virginia.

Queen Elizabeth I was wary of territorial conflict but still wanted her share of the plunder. Under her own authority and not in the name of England she financed independent explorers and traders with the intention of sharing the spoils. Known as Sea Dogs they were active starting in 1560. They committed piracy in the Caribbean, Spanish colonies as well as in European waters. They also engaged in slave trading.

Sir Francis Drake (1540–1596) and Sir Walter Raleigh (1552– 1618) were notable in this group.

The first dedicated cartographer was Samuel de Champlain. He began his explorations at the age of 20 abroad ships to Latin and South America. His quest eventually led to the search for a Northern Passage.

Between 1603 and 1635, he made 12 excursions to North America.

*Champlain's map extends from Virginia to Canada
and specifically includes Cape Cod.*

Captain John Smith was well known for his explorations and mapping of Virginia and the southern coast. He was the leader of the illfated Jamestown colony among many endeavors. *In 1630, after his sailing days were over,* Smith wrote *The True Travels, Adventures, and Observations of Captain John Smith. He was everything from a mercenary, a slave, a ship's captain, an explorer, a cartographer, governor of Virginia and love interest of Pocahontas.* John Smith's biographer, Philip L. Barbour, once wrote, "Let it only be said that nothing John Smith wrote has yet been found to be a lie."

Captain Smith arrived in Cape Cod in 1614 with several ships under his command. His purpose was to map the northern coast. He named the area New England and hoped to establish a plantation or colony.

Captain Smith left Ship's Master Thomas Hunt there to establish trade with the Indians as the first step in a permanent settlement. Hunt, however, had his own agenda. He lured 24 Nausea and Patuxent Indians onboard his ship to establish trade, but instead, took them captive.

Hunt took the Indians to Malaga, Spain, where he began selling them as slaves. When the local Friars realized the Indians had been captured in America, they interceded and began converting them to

Catholicism. There are also tales they were put in museums, rather like a human zoo.

The Nausea and Patuxent tribes were outraged by the kidnappings. Their reactions were swift and clear. Visiting ships were no longer seen as trading partners, but as enemies. There are stories of ships being taken and burned with the English crew being killed or taken as slaves.

The events intensified in 1616. First the plagues of smallpox and tuberculosis wiped out the entire village at Patuxent and then spread through the surrounding area. It would be impossible to determine which ships introduced the viruses. Small pox had wreaked havoc in Virginia and found its way to New England. A hundred or more ships had made contact over the previous decade. The virulent disease brought by the traders to Cape Cod in 1616 to 1619 is cited as smallpox. Current studies have determined that it was more likely the Black Death from Eastern Europe and Asia.

The Wampanoag's would have had no previous exposure and immunity prior to the influx of explorers, traders, fishermen, and pirates.

(The epidemic that raged in 1623 affected both the settlers from England as well as the Natives. Apparently, the English had no immunity either. One of the casualties was Thomas Blossom, the spiritual leader of the Pilgrims.)

Records of the ships bringing traders or explorers are scarce.

Interestingly, we know the stories of the ships that carried passengers.

Captain Christopher Jones and The Maps on Board the Mayflower

Captain Christopher Jones was listed as master and part owner of the Mayflower in 1609. Two years later Jones and his family moved to the South bank of the River Thames in London. Over the coming years Jones worked in the wine trade, using the Mayflower to bring wine back from France, Spain, Portugal, and the Canary Islands. In 1619 he and his ship were chartered to undertake the Pilgrim voyage across the Atlantic. Because he was an active ship owner and captain in a major port, he would have been privy to the lore and stories in his community. He undoubtedly would have owned the best maps of North America before embarking on his voyage to Virginia. When they landed in Cape Cod the maps would have clearly shown his position far north of their intended destination in Virginia.

Many believe that Plymouth was named after the Pilgrims' port of departure in Plymouth, England, but Smith was actually the first to call the site "New Plimouth" on his map four years earlier. In fact, in A Description of New England, Smith astutely noted that Plymouth was "an excellent good harbor, good land; and now want of any thing, but industrious people."

John Smith's map of North America 1616

CHAPTER 7 | PILGRIMS IN AMERICA LANDING IN CAPE COD AND THE FIRST ENCOUNTER AT SKAKET

Captain John Smith explored Provincetown harbor in 1614 and wrote:

"Cape Cod... is only a headland of high hills of sand, overgrown with shrubby pines, hurts, and such trash, but an excellent harbor for all weathers. This Cape is made by the main sea on the one side, and a great bay on the other, in form of a sickle..."

He was referring to the area now known as Provincetown Harbor. The fishermen had given this harbor the name because of the abundance of cod in these waters.

Captain Myles Standish, Stephen Hopkins, and a small scouting party began their search from the first landing site of the Mayflower in Provincetown Harbor. Captain Christopher Jones of the Mayflower would have given them access to Smith's map and notes.

Things were uneventful until they reached Skaket the site of the first encounter. Skaket was short for the Algonquin name Namskaket meaning "at the fishing place".

The scouting party heard shots from the pine bushes. The Nauset would have given warning since they had previous bad experiences with Europeans. Granted there had been fishermen, explorers, and traders who were peaceable, but there had been many horrible events. The natives had been killed, captured and exposed to disease. Since there had not previously been any settlers the Nauset would not have considered that possibility. The Pilgrims shot back. No one was hurt. It is always called a skirmish.

The Pilgrims went back to the Mayflower and sailed on. Given that they wanted to establish their own plantation to grow crops, this area would have shown little promise and the skirmish easily dissuaded them from choosing that spot. That suited the Nauset very well.

They sailed on across the bay and found the site Captain Smith had named "Plimouth." They considered this site providential.

The Pilgrim women and children lived out of the Mayflower, and ferried back and forth while the men mostly stayed on land to build their storehouses and living houses. They labored all through the winter months of December, January, February, and didn't start moving entirely to shore until March. And during that entire time, they saw almost no signs of any Indians.

During this time they were certainly being followed by the natives. The loss of lives of the Pilgrims would have been recognized as well.

SQUANTO

One of the Pawtuxet natives kidnapped by Thomas Hunt would make his mark on history. His name was Tisquantum, who later became known as "Squanto". As a sign of his extraordinary skills Tisquantum learned to speak English. He escaped imprisonment in Spain and managed to find passage to London, England where he met John Slaney who was the treasurer of the Newfoundland Company. Tisquantum was hired as an interpreter and guide spending a year working for Captain John Mason, governor of the Newfoundland Colony. Tisquantum's reputation as an effective bilingual guide was brought to the attention of beaver trader Thomas Dermer who required help with the Wampanoag. He recognized that Tisquantum, would be ideal not only as an interpreter, but also as peacemaker between the English and the increasingly hostile Indians of the Cape Cod area.

Captain Dermer and Tisquantum arrived in Cape Cod in 1619. They located Tisquantum's village and found all the Patuxet were dead from the plague. Having lost his entire community, Tisquantum made contact with Chief Massasoit, the head of the Wampanoag Nation, and lived among his tribe. Dermer had no luck making peace with the Nauset. He was attacked and taken captive. Tisquantum, acting as intermediary, came to Dermer's rescue and negotiated his release. Dermer would continue on south without Tisquantum, where he was attacked again at Martha's Vineyards. He would die of the wounds after reaching Jamestown, Virginia.

MASSASOIT

Massasoit was the leader (sachem) of the Wampanoag Nation. Trading with the Europeans had become common over the preceding decade. With it came disease that had devastated his tribe, in some cases wiping out entire villages such as the one the Pilgrims had assumed. West of the Wampanoag was the rival Narragansett Nation. Relations between the two nations were often at odds. Being further away from the coast where most of the contact with the Europeans took place had thus far spared the Narragansett from rampant disease.

The Wampanoag kept their distance from the settlers through the first winter. That spring a decision would have to be made. Massasoit fearing an attack from the much stronger Narragansett contemplated the possibility of allying with the settlers. Samoset spoke some English and was a visiting sachem of an allied Pemaquid tribe to the north. Tisquantum was back in the fold and a fluent English speaker but his years away made him an unreliable interlocutor in the mind of Massasoit. Samoset was chosen to make formal contact.

MOURT'S RELATION

Mort's Relation is a 1622 account of the early days of Plymouth Colony. It describes Samoset's initial visit thus:

Friday the 16th a fair warm day towards; this morning we determined to conclude of the military orders, which we had begun to consider of before but were interrupted by the savages, as we mentioned formerly; and whilst we were busied hereabout, we were interrupted again, for there presented himself a savage, which caused an alarm. He very boldly came all alone and along the houses straight to the rendezvous, where we intercepted him, not suffering him to go in, as undoubtedly he would, out of his boldness. He saluted us in English, and bade us welcome, for he had learned some broken English among the Englishmen that came to fish at Monchiggon, and knew by name the most of the captains, commanders, and masters that usually come. He was a man free in speech, so far as he could express his mind, and of a seemly carriage. We questioned him of many things; he was the first savage we could meet withal. He said he was not of these parts, but of Morattiggon, and one of the sagamores or lords thereof, and had been eight months in these parts, it lying hence a day's sail with a great wind, and five days by land. He discoursed of the whole country, and of every province, and of their sagamores, and their number of men, and strength. The wind being to rise a little, we cast a horseman's coat about him, for he was stark naked, only a leather about his waist, with a fringe about a span long, or little more; he had a bow and two arrows, the one headed, and the other unheaded. He was a tall straight man, the hair of his head black, long behind, only short before, none on his face at all; he asked some beer, but we gave him strong water and biscuit, and butter, and cheese, and pudding, and a piece of mallard, all which he liked well, and had been acquainted with such amongst the English. He told us the place where we now live is called Patuxet, and that about four years ago all the inhabitants died of an extraordinary plague, and there is neither man, woman, nor child remaining, as indeed we have found none, so as there is none to hinder our possession, or to lay claim unto it. All the afternoon we spent in communication with him; we would gladly have been rid of him at night, but he was not willing to go this night. Then we thought to carry him on shipboard, wherewith he was well content, and went into the shallop, but the wind was high and the water scant, that it could not return back. We lodged him that night at Stephen Hopkins' house, and watched him.

The next day he went away back to the Massasoits, from whence he said he came, who are our next bordering neighbors. They are sixty strong, as he saith. The Nausets are as near southeast of them, and are a hundred strong, and those were they of whom our people were encountered, as before related. They are much incensed and provoked against the English, and about eight months ago slew three Englishmen, and two more hardly escaped by flight to Monchiggon; they were Sir Ferdinando Gorges his men, as this savage told us, as he did likewise of the huggery, that is, fight, that our discoverers had with the Nausets, and of our tools that were taken out of the woods, which we willed him should be brought again, otherwise, we would right ourselves. These people are ill affected towards the English, by reason of one Hunt, a master of a ship, who deceived the people, and got them under color of trucking with them, twenty out of this very place where we inhabit, and seven men from Nauset, and carried them away, and sold them for slaves like a wretched man (for twenty pound a man) that cares not what mischief he doth for his profit.

Saturday, in the morning we dismissed the savage, and gave him a knife, a bracelet, and a ring; he promised within a night or two to come again, and to bring with him some of the Massasoits, our neighbors, with such beavers' skins as they had to truck with us.

On March 21 Samoset returned to the Pilgrim village as promised with Tisquantum to continue the dialog.

CHAPTER 8 | THE FIRST TREATY

*The Ceremony of the Peace Pipe was between
Massasoit and Governor John Carver.*

William Bradford's account:

Thursday, the 22nd of March, was a very fair warm day. About noon we met again about our public business, but we had scarce been an hour together, but Samoset came again, and Squanto, the only native of Patuxet, where we now inhabit, who was one of the twenty captives that by Hunt were carried away, and had been in England, and dwelt in Cornhill with Master John Slaine, a merchant, and could speak a little English, with three others, and they brought with them some few skins to truck, and some red herrings newly taken and dried, but not salted, and signified unto us that their great sagamore [chief] Massasoit was hard by, with Quadequina his brother, and all their men. They could not well express in English what they would, but after an hour the king came to the top of a hill over against us, and had in his train sixty men, that we could well behold them and they us.

We were not willing to send our governor to them, and they unwilling to come to us, so Squanto went again unto him, who brought word that we should send one to parley with him, which we did, which was Edward Winslow, to know his mind, and to signify the mind and will of our governor, which was to have trading and peace with him. We sent to the king a pair of knives, and a <u>copper</u> chain with a jewel at it. To Quadequina we sent likewise a knife and a jewel to hang in his ear, and withal a pot of strong water, a good quantity of biscuit, and some butter, which were all willingly accepted.

At this point in the story, Edward Winslow gives himself up as a hostage to ensure the safety of Massasoit. Winslow agrees to place himself in the charge of the sachem's brother Quadequina outside of the village while Massasoit and a small party enter the village to negotiate.

They saluted him and he them, so one going over, the one on the one side, and the other on the other, conducted him to a house then in building, where we placed a green rug and three or four cushions. Then instantly came our governor [John Carver] with drum and trumpet after him, and some few musketeers. After salutations, our governor kissing his hand, the king kissed him, and so they sat down. The governor called for some strong water, and drunk to him, and he drunk a great draught that made him sweat all the while after; he [Carver] called for a little fresh meat, which the king did eat willingly, and did give his followers. Then they treated of peace, which was:

> ➤ That neither he nor any of his should injure or do hurt to any of our people.
> ➤ And if any of his did hurt to any of ours, he should send the offender, that we might punish him.
> ➤ That if any of our tools were taken away when our people were at work, he should cause them to be restored, and if

ours did any harm to any of his, we would do the like to them.

> If any did unjustly <u>war</u> against him, we would aid him; if any did war against us, he should aid us.

He should send to his neighbor confederates, to certify them of this, that they might not wrong us, but might be likewise comprised in the conditions of peace.

That when their men came to us, they should leave their bows and arrows behind them, as we should do our pieces when we came to them.

Lastly, that doing thus, King James would esteem of him as his friend and ally.

All of which the king seemed to like well, and it was applauded of his followers...So after all was done, the governor conducted him to the brook, and there they embraced each other and he departed; we diligently keeping our hostages, we expected our messenger's coming, but anon, word was brought us that Quadequina was coming, and our messenger was stayed till his return, who presently came a troop with him, so likewise we entertained him, and conveyed him to the place prepared. He was very fearful of our pieces [muskets], and made signs of dislike, that they should be carried away, whereupon commandment was given they should be laid away. He was a very proper tall young man, of a very modest and seemly countenance, and he did kindly like of our entertainment, so we conveyed him likewise as we did the king, but diverse of their people stayed still. When he was returned, then they dismissed our messenger...

The next morning, diverse of their people came over to us, hoping to get some victuals as we imagined; some of them told us the king would have some of us come see him. Captain Standish and Isaac Allerton went venturously, who were welcomed of him after their manner; he gave them three or four ground-nuts and some tobacco. We cannot yet conceive but that he is willing to have peace with us, for they have seen our people sometimes alone two or three in the woods at work and fowling, when as they offered them no harm as they might easily have done, and especially because he [Massasoit] hath a potent adversary the

Narragansetts, that are at war with him, against whom he thinks we may be some strength to him, for our pieces are terrible unto them. This morning they stayed till ten or eleven of the clock, and our governor bid them send the king's kettle, and filled it full of peas, which pleased them well, and so they went their way.

The Wampanoag-Pilgrim Treaty was signed by Massasoit and Governor Carver. Several days later Captain Jones and his crew set sail for England on the Mayflower. Captain Jones had originally planned to return to England as soon as the Pilgrims found a settlement site. As his crew members began to be ravaged by the same diseases that were felling the Pilgrims, he realized that he had to remain in Plymouth Harbor "till he saw his men began to recover." Jones had lost his boatswain, his gunner, three quartermasters, the cook, and more than a dozen sailors.

Several remained to colonize. About 15 returned.

Captain Jones offered passage to anyone who wanted to return to England. Significantly, none of the Pilgrims chose to return. All were committed to their New Land.

Just two weeks later, Governor Carver died. In six months, he led the successful landing of the Mayflower after the horrendous crossing, established a permanent colony, as well as the two initial covenants: The Mayflower Compact and the Wampanoag-Pilgrim Treaty of Peace.

CHAPTER 9 | WOMEN ON THE MAYFLOWER

The Unsung Heroes and The Casualties

Nineteen women made the voyage on the Mayflower. After landing, they continued to live onboard with the teenagers and children. One can only imagine the severity of the squalor below deck. The ship was built to carry cargo, specifically wine. It was not designed to carry passengers. The cargo sections of ships were five feet high and soaked with decades of spilled wine. There were 130 people plus animals sharing this limited space for three months. One month in port in Plymouth, England and two of which were spent crossing the Atlantic encountering multiple raging storms. After the ship landed the men stayed outside in the cold. This was in fact the end of the Little Ice Age and conditions were harsh.

Dorothy Bradford was the first casualty. She died Dec 7, 1620 in port at Plymouth. She went overboard. Whether she fell or jumped is lost to history.

The Mayflower stayed anchored in the bay throughout the winter. Fourteen women did not live to see the first spring. Unsanitary conditions aboard the ship certainly contributed to severe illness. The thoughtfulness of keeping the women sheltered inside the ship was ultimately a death sentence for most of them. Only four women and two teenaged girls survived that first winter. The men living ashore generally fared better, 30 of the 52 men survived.

William Bradford's Register of Some of the First Deaths at Plymouth

Elizabeth Winslow: March 24, "Dies Elizabeth, the wife of Master Edward Winslow," Ibid., p. 38. N.B.

This month, Thirteen of our number die. And in three months past, die Half our Company. The greatest part in the depth of winter, wanting houses and other comforts; being infected with the scurvy and other diseases which their long voyage and unaccommodate condition bring upon them. So as there die sometimes two or three a day. Of one hundred persons, scarce 50 remain. The living were scarce able to bury the dead; the well not sufficient to tend the sick: there being in their time of greatest distress but six or seven who spare no pains to help them. Two of the seven were Master Brewster, their reverend Elder, and Master Standish the Captain. The like disease fell also among the sailors; so as almost Half their company also die, before they sail. (Ibid., pp. 38-39.) (Deetz, J)

After Mayflower returned to England, the four surviving women assumed domestic chores for the entire group.

1. Elizabeth Hopkins, Stephen's wife gave birth while at sea, to a boy she aptly named Oceanus. She nursed another child, whose mother had died that winter.

2. Su•sanna White gave birth to Peregrine while the ship was anchored in Cape Cod in late November 1620. She had a fiveyear-old son called Resolved. She was widowed that winter. In addition, she also nursed a baby whose mother had died. She went on to become Edward Winslow's second wife.

3. Mary Brewster, Mary Brewster, wife of the religious leader, William Brewster. Mary came to Plymouth on the *Mayflower* in 1620 with their two youngest children Love

and Wrestling. Son Jonathan Brewster joined the family in November 1621, arriving at Plymouth on the ship *Fortune*. Daughters Patience and Fear came on the ship *Anne* in 1623. One can see her as the confirming partner of a dynamic, purpose-driven man.

4. Eleanor Billington came on the Mayflower with her husband, John, and two sons, John and Francis. She is an oddity as a heroine. Her husband was executed for murder. Later, she was sentenced to sit in the stock and be whipped for a slander against John Doane. It is probably fair to say that the notion of women having equal rights had not yet taken hold. Never the less, she withstood the prejudices of the time and was married to Gregory Armstrong, living respectfully thereafter. The descendants of John and Eleanor Billington did not suffer ongoing stigma since their descendants include President Garfield. Two teenage girls assisted the four mothers.

5. Priscilla Mullins. Her parents, brother and sister died that first winter. She was eighteen years old. Her response to the proposal of marriage delivered by John Alden had the legendary response "Speak for yourself, John." They are listed as the ancestors of Presidents John and John Quincy Adams

6. Constance Hopkins, daughter of Stephen Hopkins, stepdaughter of Elizabeth Hopkins, age 15 daughter of Stephen Hopkins, step-daughter of Elizabeth Hopkins, age 15. That first spring in the new land, the colonists looked on as the two young men, Edward Doty and Edward Leister, carried on a dual courtship for the hand of pretty Constance [Hopkins]. On 18 June 1621, the colonists were awakened at dawn by the sound of the clash of cold steel. Rushing outside, they found Leister and Doty slashing away at each other in a duel.

"They were quickly disarmed and hauled before Governor Bradford, who ordered them strung up with head and heels tied together so they could cool off their hot blood." Governor Bradford said later that "Edward Doty retrieved his character by change from youthful folly."

The fair Miss Constance never married either swain. Instead, she later married the honorable <u>Nicholas Snow</u>, one of the founders of Eastham, Barnstable County, Massachusetts. (Constance (HOPKINS) SNOW).

There were no ships logs written by the women. One could have written this:

Since we docked, We women and the children have continued to live in the Ship itself. The men have done this kindly since our quarters are considered better than those outside. The men and the crew have built caves in the snow. The snow is higher than any of us and it is so very cold. They live outside and bring only the men who are sick into our ship. So we nurse them while so many women are dying as well. It seems our ship is actually an infirmary.

Today the Gorge Hurst, the cook for the crew died in our ship so we are cooking for the crew.

Dr. Giles Heale, the ship's surgeon, comes aboard to help but there is little he can do.

In reality the interior of the ship was pestilent from the beginning of the journey with raging storms when all passengers, crew and animals left excrement, orally and rectally in the living quarters. Results included scurvy, pneumonia, tuberculous, and starvation. The sanitary conditions were certainly deplorable and extensive.

The men lived stoically in makeshift shelter outside while they built homes. They were braving the harsh Little Ice Age weather while the conditions on board were actually the most serious.

Deep snow is mentioned. It is probable the men built caves carved in the mountains of snow. One could surmise that living on land in whatever conditions was preferable to staying aboard the ship. When the winter was over, about half of the passengers and half of the crew had died. The women had the highest mortality rates in that 19 out of 23 died.

They all deserve awe and gratitude.

CHAPTER 10 | THE FIRST THANKSGIVING

In the autumn of 1621 there were 52 Pilgrim survivors. They had made it to this point against daunting odds and with gratitude for the help they had received from the Wampanoag's. They had gone from starvation to ample provisions and safety.

Ninety Wampanoag's and their allies came to this first Thanksgiving. They demonstrated their full honors, showing the elevated status given to the Peace Treaty that had been signed in the spring.

This is Edward Winslow's account of the first Thanksgiving, which he wrote in a letter

Our corn [i.e. wheat] did prove well, and God be praised, we had a good increase of Indian corn, and our barley indifferent good, but our peas not worth the gathering, for we feared they were too late sown. They came up very well, and blossomed, but the sun parched them in the blossom. Our harvest being gotten in, our governor sent four men on fowling, that so we might after a special manner rejoice together after we had gathered the fruit of our labors. They four in one day killed as much fowl as, with a little help beside, served the company almost a week. At which time, amongst other recreations, we exercised our arms, many of the Indians coming amongst us, and among the rest their greatest king Massasoit, with some ninety men, whom for three days we entertained and feasted, and they went out and killed five deer, which they brought to the plantation and bestowed on our governor, and upon the captain and others. And although it be not always as plentiful as it was at this time with us, yet by the goodness of God, we are so far from want that we often wish you partakers of our plenty. (JOHNSON. C)

The second description was written about twenty years after the fact by William Bradford in his History of Plymouth Plantation. This document was rediscovered in 1854 after having been taken by British looters during the Revolutionary War. This discovery prompted a greater American interest in the history of the Pilgrims.

Bradford writes: They "fit up their houses and dwellings against winter, being all well recovered in health and strength and had all things in good plenty. For as some were thus employed in affairs abroad, others were exercising in fishing, about cod and bass and other fish, of which they took good store, of which every family had their portion. All the summer there was no want; and now began to come in store of fowl, as winter approached, of which this place did abound when they came first (but afterward decreased by degrees). And besides waterfowl there was great store of wild turkeys, of which they took many, besides venison, etc. Besides they had about a peck of meal a week to a person, or now since harvest,

Indian corn to that proportion. Which made many afterwards write so largely of their plenty here to their friends in England, which were not feigned but true reports. The primary sources above only list a few items that were on the Thanksgiving "menu", namely five deer, a large number of turkeys.

That Chief Massasoit came with 90 chiefs and braves in full regalia is very significant. His own tribe had been decimated by disease. His own leadership was in jeopardy and was likely to be challenged by the Narragansets, who had not been affected by the epidemic.

Thanksgiving was a pronouncement of his leadership and the relationship between the tribes on the mainland and the Pilgrims. His leadership was recognized by this successful event.

This first Thanksgiving did not become a tradition. It was a spontaneous celebration of survival and accomplishment. Plymouth Colony had been established, a bountiful harvest was collected and cooperation with the neighboring Wampanoag tribe was on solid footing. The idea of a brighter future was certainly implied if not explicitly so.

THE COLONIES BECOME ESTABLISHED

In 1626, King James died. His son, Charles I, became the new Stuart King of England and Scotland. He cared little to nothing of his father's religiosity. He was immediately dedicated to taxes.

Other ships followed the Mayflower with the rest of Pastor John Robinson's congregation from Leiden, Holland. Robinson died in 1626 with Thomas Blossom assuming his role as leader. The Brownists/ Pilgrim migration concluded in 1629 with a fleet of six ships, which included Blossom, joining the Plymouth Colony.

The first Puritans migrated with the Winthrop Fleet in 1630 and established the Massachusetts Bay Colony. They were Non-Separatists, Members of the Church of England. Their profile included a high percentage of lesser nobility, who were the younger sons in the primogeniture system. They had passion to make a new life devoid of the luck of birth order. Avoiding taxation by King Charles was an issue as well as opportunities in employment and professions. The Puritans, who were intensely religious, wanted to change the Church from within by eliminating rituals and practices that were Catholic in origin. Proselytizing and conversion played a large role in their church.

The Puritans espoused a God-given superiority. They did not come to America to make friends. They were aggressive came to take whatever they pleased. Their divine mission was to create a City upon a Hill in North America's New Jerusalem. The idea of a Puritan Thanksgiving as a gesture of peace and cooperation with the native tribes would not have been considered.

The Pilgrims and the Puritans had limited interaction and divergent beliefs and lifestyles in the early years. Pilgrims followed Old Testament teachings and stories. They wanted their privacy and freedom from interference. They did not proselytize. They made no attempts to convert the Merchant Adventurers or the natives. William Brewster continued to serve as the spiritual leader of the Pilgrims after the death of Thomas Blossom. He wrote a letter of welcoming to the Puritans as neighbors. He was the leader until his own death in 1640. The problem was finding a replacement. The ultimate problem was replacing Brewster and others. Harvard had been established in 1636 to train Puritan ministers and Pilgrims had not generated their own spiritual leaders. A few immigrated, such as Reverend John Hall. However, the void in trained Pilgrim ministers was a critical factor.

Known as the Great Migration, by 1640 the Puritan population in New England exceeded 21,000. The Pilgrims influence would be overwhelmed by the far larger Puritan population. The Puritans were not bound by that first peace treaty and perhaps even unaware.

The point is this: History needs the personal stories found in genealogy and genealogy needs the connection to history and the timelines. There are no stories of conflict between the Wampanoag's and the Pilgrim descendants that have been creditable in context. This leads to an immense insight about our First Thanksgiving. The conflict began when the Puritans arrived.

Our Mayflower Pilgrims and those on the next three ships were called "The First Comers." Their lives and their values led the way and include these significant milestones:

- ➤ The Mayflower Compact
- ➤ The Mayflower Signatories
- ➤ The Peace Treaty with Massasoit
- ➤ Thanksgiving Celebration

Their actions went forth as a unified, integrated group, a People, including birth, marriage and death. They lived and worked together according to the Compact. Their religious views were personal and private. This set a precedent for the Separation of Church and State in America.

The Puritans

Puritan society regularly celebrated "Thank Days". These were similar to the Pilgrim celebration in name only. For the Puritans it was a religious ritual of sorts. Faith and Repentance were considered the two fundamental aspects of Puritan religiosity. A day of Oaths and Repentance (which might include fasting) were commonly followed by a day of Thanksgiving and Gratitude for God's mercy. Local governments proclaimed Thank Days, which varied from these strict observances to Thanks for specific events and occurrences.

The custom of the Puritans and others in Colonial America was to pair a Fast Day devoted to repentance, healing and prayers followed by a Day of Thanksgiving. These observances were fairly common and held on the state and local level.

CHAPTER 11 | UNREST
IN THE COLONIES

S i2r Francis Bernard, after a successful stint as Governor of New Jersey was appointed to the same office in Massachusetts in 1759. He was placed in the unenviable position of instituting King George's policies and taxes just as the population and economic might of the colonies grew. As a hardliner, answering to the King, Bernard soon became lightening rod for the aggrieved colonists. Bernard's letters briefing London on the conditions in Boston were more alarmist than was warranted. In 1768 he warned of insurrection and soon 4000 British troops arrived exacerbating tensions.

Not all the Bostonians were predisposed to conflict. In more capable hands it is possible that the Governor of Massachusetts could have led a less antagonistic administration. Bernard was recalled to England in 1769 and the town held an impromptu celebration. In England he would become an advisor North administration on matters concerning the colonies continuing his hard line.

John Adams would later write that Bernard's "antagonistic reports" of matters in Massachusetts were instrumental in turning British government policymakers against colonial interests.

The rallying cry for our Revolution began at the Boston Tea Party: No Taxation without Representation! Actually, the taxes levied on the colonies were not excessive. They were instituted largely to pay off debts incurred in the French and Indian War. The opinion in England was that the taxes were just and would be used primarily for America's benefit.

The American leaders wanted a say in Parliament. The concept was an anathema to the landed gentry in England who were the members of Parliament. They feared the landless, low-class Londoners would follow suit and rise up if the Colonists had representation.

The situation was exacerbated by Mad King George III as he was called. His 60 year rule was a continual shift between his debilitating illness and his lucid times. He had massive mood shifts with "incessant loquacity," when foam ran out of his mouth as well as convulsions. He was kept out of the public in those periods. In his good modes, he was an understated leader, who did not interfere with Parliament. Britain became a constitutional Republic because of his low key ruler-ship.

In response to the Boston Tea Party King George perceived that leniency was to blame. He called on his representatives to "withstand every attempt to weaken or impair" royal sovereign authority anywhere. Losing the American colonies would imperil the entire British Empire.

As conflict dew nearer, popular opinion in England, and particularly by the merchant class, was that "a lasting and ruinous Civil War" should be expressly avoided.

CHAPTER 12 | THE REVOLUTIONARY WAR

I n response to the Boston Tea Party and other disloyal displays, King George instituted the Intolerable Acts in 1774. These consisted of four punitive laws meant to discipline the restive colonies into compliance. General Gates was installed as the military governor of Massachusetts and the locally elect council was disbanded.

Shots were fired at Lexington and Concord and the revolt or insurrection, depending on one's loyalties, had begun. Casualties numbered 95 Americans and 273 British soldiers.

In Philadelphia the Continental Congress appointed George Washington to create and lead the Continental Army. In a last ditch effort to stave off war, Congress adopted the Olive Branch Petition on July 5th 1775.

We, your Majesty's faithful subjects of the colonies of new Hampshire, Massachusetts bay, Rhode island and Providence Plantations, Connecticut, New York, New Jersey, Pennsylvania, the counties of New Castle, Kent, and Sussex, on Delaware, Maryland, Virginia, North Carolina, and South Carolina, in behalf of ourselves, and the inhabitants of these colonies, who have deputed us to represent them in general Congress, entreat your Majesty's gracious attention to this our humble petition.

The union between our Mother country and these colonies, and the energy of mild and just government, produced benefits so remarkably important, and afforded such an assurance of their permanency and increase, that the wonder and envy of other Nations were excited, while they beheld Great Britain riseing to a power the most extraordinary the world had ever known...

For by such arrangements as your Majesty's wisdom can form, for collecting the united sense of your American people, we are convinced your Majesty would receive such satisfactory proofs of the disposition of the colonists towards their sovereign and parent state, that the wished for opportunity would soon be restored to them, of evincing the sincerity of their professions, by every testimony of devotion becoming the most dutiful subjects, and the most affectionate colonists.

That your Majesty may enjoy a long and prosperous reign, and that your descendants may govern your dominions with honor to themselves and happiness to their subjects, is our sincere and fervent prayer.

First among the many signors was John Hancock who would famously sign the Declaration of Independence a year later.

King George responded with a proclamation of his own:

A Proclamation for Suppressing Rebellion and Sedition

WHEREAS Many of Our Subjects in divers Parts of Our Colonies and Plantations in North America, misled by dangerous and illdesigning Men, and forgetting the Allegiance which they owe to the Power that has protected and sustained them, after various disorderly Acts committed in Disturbance of the Public Peace, to the Obstruction of lawful Commerce, and to the Oppression of Our loyal Subjects carrying on the same, have at length proceeded to an open and avowed Rebellion, by arraying themselves in hostile Manner to withstand the Execution of the Law, and traitoursly preparing, ordering, and levying War against Us.

British Prime Minister Lord North followed through and issued military reinforcements to squash the rebellion.

Thousands of rebel militia converged to attack the British garrison in Boston and were met by General Howe. Howe's men cleared the

Americans from the high ground in the Battle of Bunker Hill at great cost. The rebels had been repelled but they had been energized and there was no turning back.

Perhaps there is nothing quite so American as antipathy toward taxes. The Continental Congress was tasked with waging a war but had no authority to raise taxes to pay for it. They essentially relied on asking the states for donations. Washington's army was thusly notoriously underpaid and poorly equipped throughout the war. Additionally, British naval supremacy conferred a great strategic advantage.

Battles were waged in New England, upstate New York and North Carolina with both sides claiming victories.

In the Spring of 1776, Congress had acted to separate itself from British rule offering "that these United Colonies are, and of right ought to be, free and independent States". In Philadelphia, Congress passed "The Unanimous Declaration of the Thirteen United States of America." in July of 1776.

The British arrived in New York that same week with a massive fleet and 34,000 troops. Their mission was to crush the rebellion and demand capitulation. Washington's forces were no match but he did manage to somewhat miraculously evacuate New York with his army intact. For the next several months the British chased Washington's army in a series of battles. None proved decisive and Washington managed to escape, albeit with an increasingly haggard force.

1777

Fast forwarding to the Autumn of 1777, General Gates aided by heroic actions of Benedict Arnold defeated the British in three pivotal battles at Saratoga, New York. British General Burgoyne was forced to surrender when promised reinforcements did not appear.

This was a major turning point in the Revolutionary War. It offered the possibility that Americans could win and led to a greater alliance and involvement by the French in support of the patriot's cause. The Continental Congress asked General Washington to proclaim a Day of Thanks to celebrate the victory. Thus, December 18, 1777 was the first official National Day of Thanksgiving. The Continental Congress made similar recommendations through 1784.

George Washington was unlikely to know of the Pilgrim's Thanksgiving celebration specifically. As mentioned previously, in puritanical New England, a Day of Repentance and Humiliation followed by a Day of Thanks was a familiar religious ritual. This celebration was a departure from that.

As an aside, Benedict Arnold felt his actions in victory were overlooked. He had been passed up for promotions and had offered his resignation before being ordered to serve under rival Gates. In the heat of battle, he defied Gates' order and led a decisive charge on horseback against the British where he was wounded. This perceived slight by the imperious Arnold led to his traitorous switch of allegiance for which he is infamously known.

*These Thank Days were the precedent Washington set as
the first President of the United States of America.*

GULPH MILLS

Just after his election in 2020, President-Elect Joe Biden gave a Thanksgiving Speech. In it he mentioned this event by then General George Washington to his troops as they were leaving to Valley Forge. At Gulph Mills, Washington addressed his troops, offering his thanks for their "fortitude and patience," promising that if they only persevered, they would achieve "the end of our Warfare: Independence, Liberty and Peace." Two days later, on Friday, December 19, 1777, the army began to march into Valley Forge.

The story accompanying the new marker is as follows:

"On December 11, 1777, the American army under General George Washington deemed their position at Whitemarsh too close to the occupied city of Philadelphia and began to move to a more defensible winter encampment. They stopped for a few days at Swedes' ford, on the north side of the Schuylkill River, but that location also was unacceptable to the American commanders. They worried that British troops might attempt raids along the Philadelphia-Lancaster turnpike, attempting to harass or capture the Continental Congress which had fled Philadelphia, passing through Lancaster before ending up in temporary quarters at York.

The army then spent nearly a week at Gulph Mills, on the other side of the river, before shifting a few miles down the road to the higher ground of the village at Valley Forge, where they remained until springtime.

Hyam Solomon

HAYM SALOMON

Haym Salomon was a Polish born Jew who immigrated to New York City. He made his fortune as an entrepreneur and trader who brokered deals between European and American interests. He belonged to the New York branch of the Sons of Liberty, a Masonic Lodge. They led the Boston Tea party rebellion against the Stamp Act. He is also listed with the Maryland Lodge No.2, Ancient York Rite.

At Valley Forge, Washington was ready to cede victory to the English. The frigid and damp winter had left his troops threadbare and starving. One evening while walking the camp, he saw Haym Salomon, a practicing Jew, lighting the Chanukah candles. Salomon had made a vast fortune since coming to the colonies. His contributions to fund the revolution were exceeded only by Robert Morris. He helped Morris secure loans for the war from France and Holland. He also used his fortune to support leaders, who did not have personal funds to cover their own needs. Included in this group were Thomas Jefferson and James Madison. Their extraordinary generosity made the revolution possible. In the end, they both died penniless.(Federer, W.)

The ever-curious Washington asked Salomon to explain his candles.

In the second century BCE, the Holy Land was ruled by the SyrianGreeks. They were dedicated to forcing the Jews to accept Greek culture and beliefs instead of the most sacred observance and belief in Gd. Against all odds, Judah the Maccabee led a small band of faithful Jews against these Greeks, one of the mightiest armies on earth. The Maccabees prevailed and drove the Greeks from the land. They reclaimed and rededicated the Holy Temple in Jerusalem.

When they sought to light the Temple's Menorah (the sevenbranched candelabrum), they found only a single container of olive oil that had not been contaminated. Miraculously, they lit the Menorah and the one-day supply of oil lasted for eight nights. Since that special time, the Festival of Chanukah has been observed each year.

Washington was so inspired by the story of a small group vanquishing the many that he opted not to surrender to the British and end the revolution. He took the story of Chanukah as a parallel situation for his troops.

Indeed, this story became an inspiration for Washington to continuing the battle against superior forces.

The story of Washington and Salomon is signified in the practical aspect of our Great Seal approved in 1783 after the Revolutionary War ended. Most of the symbols reflect the number thirteen as the higher dimension of twelve. Washington wanted also to include the Chanukah Menorah and the story by Haym Salomon. Thus, the nine tail feathers have a unique significance in our symbols.

Turn the back of our dollar bill or the front of our Great Seal upside down to see tail feathers. In this position the tail feathers represent the candles on the Menorah. The eight candles represent the nights the lights kept burning until sacred oil could be attained. The ninth candle, called the Shamash, is used to light the other eight.

The remaining years of the Revolutionary War saw victories and setbacks for both sides. Washington had to contend with his army being underfinanced leading to mutinies in 1780 & 1781. A significant population remained loyal to the King and served to disadvantage the rebels when possible. Knowing whom could be trusted was always an issue. Until the very end Washington's greatest victory was the survival of the Continental Army.

BRITISH PERSPECTIVE

The colonies were not King George's only concern. In between his bouts of madness he had domestic issues, proxy wars with France & Spain around the globe and ever present European conflicts to contend with. The colonies were just one of many territories of the growing British Empire. At the close of the French and Indian War in 1763, King

George wary of the expense required to defend huge portions on North

America, stated that England would not defend colonies west of the Appalachian Mountains. Enacting taxes on the colonies to finance its defense was met with opposition. Taking punitive measures to ensure compliance did not go well.

When violence broke out King George was aware of the disadvantages of conducting a war 3000 miles away over territory 6 times greater than England with 1000 miles of coastline. Communication and supply lines required a 75 day trans-Atlantic voyage. Never-the-less he took a hard line and declared:

> *"Blows must decide whether they are to be subject to this country, or to be independent."*

The colonies had ragtag militias without any professional army or navy to speak of. Early British successes gave way to a stalemate of sorts. Conducting a war as it was generally conducted in the 18th Century against a guerrilla tactics proved difficult. In 1778 Britain developed a Southern Strategy and took control most of Georgia and South Carolina. Pressure would test how tightly unified the states were and how committed to the cause. Early gains were short lived giving way to losses at the hands of hit and run militia.

The war reached its conclusion at Yorktown, Virginia in October 1781 when General Cornwallis was trapped and outnumbered by Washington's army, aided by the French navy. Independence was won and was ratified in the Treaty of Paris 1783.

Patriots and Loyalists

The populace was split between Patriots, Loyalists and most of all neutral "fence sitters". Pressure to sway public opinion was made by both sides. Common Sense written by Thomas Paine is the most famous of those efforts.

Britain considered the conflict a civil war but unlike the Civil War of the 19th century that had strong regional divisions these hostilities had both sides living in the same communities. Tension and animosity between the groups was high. Loyalists were harassed, had their property seized and were subjected to brutal tar and feathering. In areas controlled by Loyalists a Patriot could be accused of spying and face the gallows.

During the Revolutionary War, Washington had strong support from Jews, particularly those who were freemasons. There were Jewish soldiers at every level from foot soldiers to commanders. Of particular importance were Jews, who had their personal connections to serve as a great network of spies. Because of the long history from the Magna Carta in 1295, they needed to know those whom they could trust. Thus, they knew those, who were Loyalists, and those, who were Patriots. Particularly important were the Innkeepers, financial leaders and Rabbis.

Rabbi Gershom Mendes Sexias, leader of the Portuguese Synagogue in New York, was considered the most valuable to Washington in this intelligence gathering network.

After the war many Loyalist families of means fled to Canada and England.

ELIAS BOUDINOT

Elias Boudinot was the President of the Continental Congress at the end of the American Revolutionary War. He signed the treaty to end the war on September 3, 1783. His term was filled with many treaties and financial negotiations, domestic and foreign as well as with the Native Americans.

Boudinot directed the Secretary of War to negotiate a cease-fire with hostile Native American nations and signed the resolve:

> *Resolved, That no person or persons, citizens of these United States, or any particular State in the union in their separate capacity, can or ought to purchase any unappropriated lands belonging to the Indians without the bounds of their respective states, under any pretense whatsoever.*

Our Great Seal was ratified during his term. He was a Huguenot, a French Protestant. Importantly, he was a strong leader for the education of slaves. Realization the slaves from Africa could be taught to read and write was a new concept avidly advanced by the Quakers. Boudinot, his father and their neighbor, Benjamin Franklin, became passionate advocates for educating the Blacks and Native Americans. Years later he was a founder of The American Bible Society. It seems quite fitting that he would be the person who ultimately introduce the Articles for a Day of Thanksgiving.

CHAPTER 13 | WASHINGTON'S INAUGURATION

On April 30, 1789. George Washington was sworn in as the first President of the United States. He marched in a procession to the Senate Chamber of Federal Hall in the then-capitol of New York City. He famously swore his oath on the balcony.

Rabbi Sexias was given a prominent position. There are two versions. Both are possible. As the official spiritual representative of the Jewish citizenry, the rabbi marched in the procession of local clergy that preceded the ceremony at New York's Federal Hall. In addition, as the official representative of the State of New York, he was in the group on the balcony.

After the Oath, President Washington turned to the Rabbi and said: "I want to have a day of Thanksgiving and Celebration. It must not be religious." They agreed that Sunday and Saturday were out. Friday was out because of the Turks." They agreed it should be on a Thursday. Thus, this story tells the very first thought Washington expressed after taking his Oath of Office was to show gratitude for the beginning of our new nation.

In 1789, Elias Boudinot was elected to the House of Representatives in the first Congress. On September 24, 1789, the House of Representatives voted to recommend the First Amendment of the newly drafted Constitution to the states for ratification. The next day, Congressman Elias Boudinot proposed that the House and Senate jointly request of President Washington to proclaim a day of thanksgiving for "the many signal favors of Almighty God." Boudinot said that he could not think of letting the session finish without offering an opportunity to all the citizens of the United States of joining, with one voice, in returning to Almighty God their sincere thanks for the many blessings he had poured down upon them.

From Washington Papers, there is this account "Thanksgiving Proclamation:

"On 25 September 1789, Elias Boudinot of Burlington, New Jersey, introduced in the United States House of Representatives a resolution "That a joint committee of both Houses be directed to wait upon the President of the United States, to request that he would recommend to the people of the United States a day of public thanksgiving and prayer to be observed by acknowledging, with grateful hearts, the many signal favors of Almighty God, especially by affording them an opportunity peaceably to establish a Constitution of government for their safety and happiness."

The House was not unanimous in its determination to give thanks. Aedanus Burke of South Carolina objected that he "did not like this mimicking of European customs, where they made a mere mockery of thanksgivings."

Thomas Tudor Tucker "thought the House had no business to interfere in a matter which did not concern them. Why should the President direct the people to do what, perhaps, they have no mind to do? They may not be inclined to return thanks for a Constitution until they have experienced that it promotes their safety and happiness. We do not yet know but they may have reason to be dissatisfied with the effects it has already produced; but whether this be so or not, it is a business with which Congress have nothing to do; it is a religious matter, and, as such, is proscribed to us. If a day of thanksgiving must take place, let it be done by the authority of the several States." [1]

The Continental Thanksgiving celebration was passed by the House. A committee consisting of Elias Boudinot, Roger Sherman, and

Peter Silvester was appointed to approach President Washington. The Senate agreed to the resolution on 26 September and appointed William Samuel Johnson and Ralph Izard to the joint committee. On 28 September the Senate committee reported that they had laid the resolution before the president.

Thanksgiving Proclamation By President Washington New York, 3 October 1789

By the President of the United States of America. A Proclamation.

Whereas it is the duty of all Nations to acknowledge the providence of Almighty God, to obey his will, to be grateful for his benefits, and humbly to implore his protection and favor—and whereas both Houses of Congress have by their joint Committee requested me "to recommend to the People of the United States a day of public thanksgiving and prayer to be observed by acknowledging with grateful hearts the many signal favors of Almighty God especially by affording them an opportunity peaceably to establish a form of government for their safety and happiness."

Now therefore I do recommend and assign Thursday the 26th day of

November next to be devoted by the People of these States to the service of that great and glorious Being, who is the beneficent Author of all the good that was, that is, or that will be—That we may then all unite in rendering unto him our sincere and humble thanks—for his kind care and protection of the People of this Country previous to their becoming a Nation—for the signal and manifold mercies, and the favorable interpositions of his Providence which we experienced in the course and conclusion of the late war—for the great degree of tranquility, union, and plenty, which we have since enjoyed—for the peaceable and rational manner, in which we have been enabled to establish constitutions of government for our safety and happiness, and particularly the national One now lately instituted—for the civil and religious liberty with which we are blessed; and the means we have of acquiring and diffusing useful knowledge; and in general for all the great and various favors which he hath been pleased to confer upon us and also that we may then unite in most humbly offering our prayers and supplications to the great Lord and Ruler of Nations and beseech him to pardon our national and other transgressions—to enable us all, whether in public or private stations, to perform our several and relative duties properly and punctually—to render our national government a blessing to all the people, by constantly being a Government of wise, just, and constitutional laws, discreetly and faithfully executed and obeyed—to protect and guide all Sovereigns and Nations (especially such as have shewn kindness unto us) and to bless them with good government, peace, and concord—To promote the knowledge and practice of true religion and virtue, and the increase of science among them and us—and generally to grant unto all Mankind such a degree of temporal prosperity as he alone knows to be best. Given under my hand at the City of New-York the third day of October in the year of our Lord 1789.

Go Washington

Washington enclosed this Thanksgiving Proclamation in his Circular to the Governors of the States, written at New York on 3 October 1789: "I do myself the honor to enclose to your Excellency a Proclamation for a general Thanksgiving which I must request the favor of you to have published and made known in your State in the way and manner that shall be most agreeable to yourself."(Says, A,)

Among the first to respond was Rabbi Sexias, who had the first conversation with Washington on his Day of Inauguration.

Rabbi Gershom Mendes Sexias Thanksgiving Proclamation of 1789

"I do recommend and assign Thursday, the 26th day of November next, to be devoted by the people of these States to the service of that great and glorious Being who is the beneficent author of all the good that was, that is, or that will be; that we may then all unite in rendering unto Him our sincere and humble thanks for His kind care and protection of the people of this country previous to their becoming a nation; for the signal and manifold mercies and the favorable interpositions of His providence in the course and conclusion of the late war; for the great degree of tranquility, union, and plenty which we have since enjoyed; for the peaceable and rational manner in which we have been unable to establish constitutions of government for our safety and happiness, and particularly the national one now lately instituted for the civil and religious liberty with which we are blessed, and the means we have of acquiring and diffusing useful knowledge; and, in general, for all the great and various favors which He has been pleased to confer upon us. (Stoked)

Washington's Great Experiment

Catharine Saw Bridge Macaulay was a prominent British author and historian who among other things championed American independence. She had the occasion to visit Mount Vernon on a trip to America in 1784 and continued a correspondence with Washington. It was evident even in the moment that this was history in the making. Their letters were certainly written with the expectation that they would be read by generations of historians as well as the intended recipient. Even so, Washington seems genuinely enthusiastic about the future of his fledgling country. The onus of war is behind and the system of government they have created is performing well in its early stages.

Madam,

Your obliging letter, dated in October last, has been received; and, as I do not know when I shall have more Leisure than at present to throw together a few observations in return for yours, I take up my Pen to do it by this early occasion.

In the first place, I thank you for your congratulatory sentiments on the event which has placed me at the head of the American Government; as well as for the indulgent partiality, which it is to be feared however, may have warped your judgment too much in my favor. But you do me no more than Justice, in supposing that, if I had been permitted to indulge my first & fondest wish, I should have remained in a private Station. Although, neither the present age or Posterity may possibly give me full credit for the feelings which I have experienced on this subject; yet I have a consciousness, that nothing short of an absolute conviction of duty could ever have brought me upon the scenes of public life again. The establishment of our new Government seemed to be the last great experiment, for promoting human happiness, by reasonable compact, in civil Society. It was to be, in the first instance, in a considerable degree, a government of increase as well as a government of Laws. Much was to be done by prudence, much by conciliation, much by firmness. Few, who are not philosophical Spectators, can realise the difficult and delicate part which a man in my situation had to act. All see, and most admire, the glare which hovers round the external trappings of elevated Office. To me, there is nothing in it, beyond the lustre which may be reflected from its connection with a power of promoting human felicity. In our progress towards political happiness my station is new; and, if I may use the expression, I walk on untrodden ground. There is scarcely any action, whose motives may not be subject to a double interpretation. There is scarcely any part of my conduct wch may not hereafter be drawn into precedent. Under such a view of the duties inherent to my arduous office, I could not but feel a diffidence in myself on the one hand; and an anxiety for the Community that every new arrangement should be made in the best possible manner on the other. If after all my humble but faithful endeavours to advance the felicity of my Country & Mankind; I may endulge a hope that my labours have not been altogether without success, it will be the only real compensation I can receive in the closing Scenes of life.

On the actual situation of this Country, under its new Government, I will, in the next place, make a few remarks. That the Government, though not absolutely perfect, is one of the best in the World, I have little doubt. I always believed that an unequivocally free & equal Representation of the People in the Legislature; together with an efficient & responsable Executive were the great Pillars on which the preservation of American Freedom must depend. It was indeed next to a Miracle that there should have been so much unanimity, in points of such importance, among such a number of Citizens, so widely scattered and so different in their habits in many respects, as the Americans were. Nor are the growing unanimity and ncreaseg good will of the Citizens to the Government less remarkable than favorable circumstances. So far as we have gone with the new Government (and it is completely organized and in operation) we have had greater reason than the most sanguine could expect to be satisfied with its success. Perhaps a number of accidental circumstances have concurred with the real effects of the Government to make the People uncommonly well pleased with their situation and prospects. The harvests of Wheat have been remarkably good—the demand for that article from abroad is great—the ncrease of Commerce is visible in every Port—and the number of new

Manufactures introduced in one year is astonishing. I have lately made a tour through the Eastern States. I found the Country, in a great degree, recovered from the ravages of War—the Towns flourishing—& the People delighted with a government instituted by themselves & for their own good. The same facts I have also reason to believe, from good authority, exist in the Southern States.

By what I have just observed, I think you will be persuaded that the ill-boding Politicians, who prognosticated that America would never enjoy any fruits from her Independence & that She would be obliged to have recourse to a foreign Power for protection, have at least been mistaken. I shall sincerely rejoice to see that the American Revolution has been productive of happy consequences on both sides of the Atlantic. The renovation of the French Constitution is indeed one of the most wonderful events in the history of Mankind: and the agency of the Marquis de la Fayette in a high degree honorable to his character. My greatest fear has been, that the Nation would not be sufficiently cool & moderate in making arrangements for the security of that liberty, of which it seems to be fully possessed.

Mr Warville, the French Gentleman you mention, has been in America & at Mount Vernon; but has returned, sometime since to France.

Mrs Washington is well and desires her Compliments may be presented to you. We wish the happiness of your fire side; as we also long to enjoy that of our own at Mount Vernon. Our wishes, you know, were limited; and I think that our plans of living will now be deemed reasonable by the considerate part of our species. Her wishes coincide with my own as to simplicity of dress, and every thing which can tend to support propriety of character without partaking of the follies of luxury and ostentation. I am with great regard Madam. Your Most Obedient and Most Humble Servant

Go: Washington

Second Thanksgiving Proclamation

Washington made one other Thanksgiving Proclamation. It was delivered as the first act in his last year as President. In the proclamation, his awareness of the status of our country is well stated as are his inspirational expressions of gratitude. His moral code is well considered.

However, he makes known his fervent considerations for acts that would undermine all that had begun.

He was adamant against getting involved in foreign wars. His last two years would focus on avoiding conflicts that were between France and Britain. He looked upon such connections with restraint and made it known in his Proclamation. Known as the Great Rule, Washington's doctrine called for avoiding foreign wars as well as treaties that could lead to wars. The French, with Thomas Jefferson's encouragement, hoped to enlist the US in its battles against England. Washington knowing the stability and perhaps success of the new government depended on foreign trade refused involvement. The US would engage in commerce with the rest of the world but not involve itself politically. Washington's Great Rule was a guiding light for the next 150 years. The Great War and World War II were avoided for as long as possible. (Treaties, alliances and foreign intervention have become the norm post WWII).

A Day of Public Thanksgiving
January 01, 1795
By the President of the United States of America

A Proclamation

When we review the calamities which afflict so many other nations. The present condition of the United States affords much matter of consolation and satisfaction. Our exemption hitherto from foreign war, an increasing prospect of the continuance of that exemption, the great degree of internal tranquility we have enjoyed, the recent confirmation of that tranquility by the suppression of an insurrection which so wantonly threatened it, the happy course of our public affairs in general, the unexampled prosperity of all classes of our citizens, are circumstances which peculiarly mark our situation with indications of the Divine beneficence toward us. In such a state of things it is in an especial manner our duty as a people, with devout reverence and affectionate gratitude, to acknowledge our many and great obligations to Almighty God and to implore Him to continue and confirm the blessings we experience.

Deeply penetrated with this sentiment, I, George Washington, President of the United States, do recommend to all religious societies and denominations, and to all persons whomsoever, within the United States to set apart and observe Thursday, the 19th day of February next, as a day of public thanksgiving and prayer, and on that day to meet together and render their sincere and hearty thanks to the Great Ruler of Nations for the manifold and signal mercies which distinguish our lot as a nation, particularly for the possession of constitutions of government which unite and by their union establish liberty with order; for the preservation of our peace, foreign and domestic; for the seasonable control which has been given to a spirit of disorder in the suppression of the late insurrection, and generally, for the prosperous course of our affairs, public and private; and at the same time humbly and fervently to beseech the kind Author of these blessings graciously to prolong them to us; to imprint on our hearts a deep and solemn sense of our obligations to Him for them; to teach us rightly to estimate their immense value; to preserve us from the arrogance of prosperity, and from hazarding the advantages we enjoy by delusive pursuits; to dispose us to merit the continuance of His favors by not abusing them; by our gratitude for them, and by a correspondent conduct as citizens and men; to render this country more and more a safe and propitious asylum for the unfortunate of other countries; to extend among us true and useful knowledge; to diffuse and establish habits of sobriety, order, morality, and piety, and finally, to impart all the blessings we possess, or ask for ourselves, to the whole family of mankind.

In testimony whereof I have caused the seal of the United States of America to be affixed to these presents, and signed the same with my hand. Done at the city of Philadelphia, the 1st day of January 1795, and of the Independence of the United States of America the nineteenth.

GO. WASHINGTON.

By the President:

EDM: RANDOLPH.

In Washington's farewell address after 8 years in officer he reiterated the primary theme of his Thanksgiving proclamation.

The great rule of conduct for us, in regard to foreign nations, is in extending our commercial relations, to have with them as little political connection as possible. Europe has a set of primary interests, which to us have none, or a very remote relation. Hence she must be engaged in frequent controversies the causes of which are essentially foreign to our concerns. Hence, therefore, it must be unwise in us to implicate ourselves, by artificial ties, in the ordinary vicissitudes of her politics, or the ordinary combinations and collisions of her friendships or enmities… it is our true policy to steer clear of permanent alliances with any portion of the foreign world.

CHAPTER 14 | THANKSGIVING AFTER WASHINGTON

JOHN ADAMS

A dams was a product of his New England upbringing with rigid practices. His Patrilineal descent in America is as follows:

1. Henry Adams emigrated from <u>Braintree</u>, Essex, in England to <u>Massachusetts Bay Colony</u> in about 1638
2. Joseph Adams Sr. (1626–1694),
3. Joseph Adams Jr. (1654–1737),
4. John Adams Sr (Deacon John) was a British colonial farmer and minister.
5. <u>President John Adams (Jr.)</u>
6. President <u>John Quincy Adams</u>.

He was also descended from John Alden and Priscilla Mullins, who came on the Mayflower through his Grandmother Hannah Bass. His ancestors were a fine list of colonists.

His patrilineal ancestry was solidly devoted to the Puritan cause. The adjective puritanical might well be used for him.

President Washington deliberately wanted to avoid religion and fast days when he chose Thursday for our day of National Thanksgiving. President Adams was unwavering in his dedication to the New England Puritan precepts.

FAST DAY PROCLAMATION

by President John Adams 28 March 1798.

As the safety and prosperity of nations ultimately and essentially depend on the protection and the blessing of Almighty God; and the national acknowledgment of this truth is not only an indispensable duty which the People owe to Him, but a duty whose natural influence is favorable to the promotion of that Morality and Piety, without which social Happiness cannot exist nor the Blessings of a Free Government be enjoyed; and as this Duty, at all times incumbent, is so especially in seasons of Difficulty or of Danger, when existing or threatening Calamities, the just Judgments of God against prevalent Iniquity, are a loud call to Repentance and Reformation: And as the United States of America are, at present, placed in a hazardous and afflictive situation, by the unfriendly Disposition, Conduct and Demands of a foreign power, evinced by repeated refusals to receive our Messengers of Reconciliation and Peace, by Depredations on our Commerce, and the Infliction of Injuries on very many of our Fellow-Citizens, while engaged in their lawful Business on the Seas:—Under these considerations it has appeared to me that the Duty of imploring the Mercy and Benediction of Heaven on our Country demands, at this time, a special attention from its Inhabitants.

I HAVE therefore thought fit to recommend, and I do hereby recommend, that Wednesday the Ninth Day of May next be observed throughout the United States, as a day of Solemn Humiliation, Fasting and Prayer: That the Citizens of these States, abstaining on that Day from their customary Worldly Occupations, offer their devout Addresses to the Father of Mercies, agreeably to those forms or methods which they have severally adopted as the most suitable and becoming: That all Religious Congregations do, with the deepest Humility, acknowledge before God the manifold Sins and Transgressions with which we are justly chargeable as Individuals and as a Nation; beseeching him, at the same time, of his infinite Grace, through the Redeemer of the World, freely to remit all our Offences, and to incline us, by his Holy Spirit, to that sincere Repentance and Reformation which may afford us reason to hope for his inestimable Favour and Heavenly Benediction: That it be made the subject of particular and earnest supplication, that our Country may be protected from all the dangers which threaten it; that our Civil and Religious privileges may be preserved inviolate and perpetuated to the latest Generations; that our public Councils and Magistrates may be especially enlightened and directed at this critical period; that the American People may be united in those Bonds of Amity and mutual Confidence, and inspired with that Vigour and Fortitude by which they have in times past been so highly distinguished, and by which they have obtained such invaluable Advantages: That the Health of the Inhabitants of our Land may be preserved, and their Agriculture, Commerce, Fisheries, Arts, and Manufactures be blessed and prospered; that the principles of Genuine Piety and Sound Morality may influence the Minds and govern the Lives of every description of our Citizens;

and that the Blessings of Peace, Freedom, and Pure Religion, may be speedily extended to all the Nations of the Earth.

And finally I recommend, that on the said day, the Duties of Humiliation and Prayer be accompanied by fervent Thanksgiving to the Bestower of every Good Gift, not only for having hitherto protected and preserved the People of these United States in the independent Enjoyment of their Religious and Civil Freedom, but also for having prospered them in a wonderful progress of Population, and for conferring on them many and great Favours conducive to the Happiness and Prosperity of a Nation.

GIVEN under my Hand and the Seal of the United States of America, at Philadelphia, this twenty-third day of March, in the Year of Our Lord one thousand seven hundred and ninety-eight, and of the Independence of the said States the twenty-second.

John Adams.

John Adams

Adams' text clearly adhered to the most puritanical concepts. It followed rigid precepts and practices. The Original Sin interpretation of story in the Garden of Eden predominated his entire statement. His religiosity is so tightly ingrained that he has no concept of the separation of church and state. He says it all when he speaks of "One True Religion."

THOMAS JEFFERSON

Thomas Jefferson was outraged. He was adamant that concepts violated the separation of Church and State. He expressed his views in response to a Baptist group, stating that he believed in "a wall of separation between Church and State." In a draft, he was more explicit, He declared fasts or days of thanksgiving to be expressions of religion and that he opposed them because they were remnants of Britain's reign over the American colonies.(Blakemore, E)

"I consider the government of the US. as interdicted by the constitution from intermedling with religious institutions, their doctrines, discipline, or exercises. this results not only from the provision that no law shall be made respecting the establishment, or free exercise, of religion, but from that also which reserves to the states the powers not delegated to the US. Certainly no power to prescribe any religious exercise, or to assume authority in religious discipline, has been delegated to the general government. it must then rest with the states, as far as it can be in any human authority...I do not believe it is for the interest of religion to invite the civil magistrate to direct it's exercises, its discipline or its doctrines: nor of the religious societies that the General government should be invested with the power of effecting any uniformity of time or matter among them. Fasting & prayer are religious exercises. the enjoining them an act of discipline, every religious society has a right to determine for itself the times for these exercises & the objects proper for them according to their own particular tenets. And this right can never be safer than in their own hands, where the constitution has deposited it..., Civil powers alone have been given to the President of the US. and no authority to direct the religious exercises of his constituents. (Jefferson, T)

It was a major point of contention between Adams and Jefferson and their differences became quite heated. Years later when they became reconciled, Adams said this issue broke his possibility for a second term.

President Jefferson did not follow the lead of the first two presidents. He continued his passionate stance against federal Thanksgiving and for the Separation of Church and State. Interestingly, he took a position in favor of Thanksgiving from the context of the states, both before and after his presidency.

JAMES MADISON

President James Madison, the Fourth President of the United States of America established that our victory against Britain was valid and durable in the international arena. United States of America was accepted and established by our victory in the War of 1812.

Madison issued two Proclamations aligned to the precepts of

Adams. These were given in the light of that given by Washington after defeating the British in our revolution. They were given in 1814 and 1815 subsequent to the War of 1812.

Proclamation 18—Recommending a Day of Public Humiliation, Fasting, and Prayer

November 16, 1814
By the President of the United States of America
A Proclamation

The two Houses of the National Legislature having by a joint resolution expressed their desire that in the present time of public calamity and war a day may be recommended to be observed by the people of the United States as a day of public humiliation and fasting and of prayer to Almighty God for the safety and welfare of these States, His blessing on their arms, and a speedy restoration of peace, I have deemed it proper by this proclamation to recommend that Thursday, the 12th of January next, be set apart as a day on which all may have an opportunity of voluntarily offering at the same time in their respective religious assemblies their humble adoration to the Great Sovereign of the Universe, of confessing their sins and transgressions, and of strengthening their vows of repentance and amendment. They will be invited by the same solemn occasion to call to mind the distinguished favors conferred on the American people in the general health which has been enjoyed, in the abundant fruits of the season, in the progress of the arts instrumental to their comfort, their prosperity, and their security, and in the victories which have so powerfully contributed to the defense and protection of our country, a devout thankfulness for all which ought to be mingled with their supplications to the Beneficent Parent of the Human Race that He would be graciously pleased to pardon all their offenses against Him; to support and animate them in the discharge of their respective duties; to continue to them the precious advantages flowing from political institutions so auspicious to their safety against dangers from abroad, to their tranquillity at home, and to their liberties, civil and religious; and that He would in a special manner preside over the nation in its public councils and constituted authorities, giving wisdom to its measures and success to its arms in maintaining its rights and in overcoming all hostile designs and attempts against it; and, finally, that by inspiring the enemy with dispositions favorable to a just and reasonable peace its blessings may be speedily and happily restored.

Given at the city of Washington, the 16th day of November, 1814, and of the Independence of the United States the thirty-eighth.

JAMES MADISON.

Proclamation 20—Recommending a Day of Public Thanksgiving for Peace

March 04, 1815
By the President of the United States of America
A Proclamation

The Senate and House of Representatives of the United States have by a joint resolution signified their desire that a day may be recommended to be observed by the people of the United States with religious solemnity as a day of thanksgiving and of devout acknowledgments to Almighty God for His great goodness manifested in restoring to them the blessing of peace.

No people ought to feel greater obligations to celebrate the goodness of the Great Disposer of Events and of the Destiny of Nations than the people of the United States. His kind providence originally conducted them to one of the best portions of the dwelling place allotted for the great family of the human race. He protected and cherished them under all the difficulties and trials to which they were exposed in their early days. Under His fostering care their habits, their sentiments, and their pursuits prepared them for a transition in due time to a state of independence and self-government. In the arduous struggle by which it was attained they were distinguished by multiplied tokens of His benign interposition. During the interval which succeeded He reared them into the strength and endowed them with the resources which have enabled them to assert their national rights and to enhance their national character in another arduous conflict, which is now so happily terminated by a peace and reconciliation with those who have been our enemies. And to the same Divine Author of Every Good and Perfect Gift we are indebted for all those privileges and advantages, religious as well as civil, which are so richly enjoyed in this favored land.

It is for blessings such as these, and more especially for the restoration of the blessing of peace, that I now recommend that the second Thursday in April next be set apart as a day on which the people of every religious denomination may in their solemn assemblies unite their hearts and their voices in a freewill offering to their Heavenly Benefactor of their homage of thanksgiving and of their songs of praise.

Given at the city of Washington on the 4th day of March, A. D. 1815, and of the Independence of the United States the thirty- ninth.

JAMES MADISON.

Madison's Proclamations follow the first proclamation by President Washington in straightforward gratitude after the success of winning independence and establishing our new federal government. Madison' first proclamation follows the Puritan approach of fast and repentance followed by Thanksgiving. His second shows the shift eliminating the context of humility and repentance.

He announces by Recommending "PUBLIC THANKSGIVING FOR PEACE." He clearly establishes Washington's Gratitude as well as the separation of Church and State.

The concept of Thanksgiving as a national holiday did not go forth. There were state and local celebrations without a national connection, a unified theme or a common date.

CHAPTER 15 | A STEP BACK TO THE FOUNDING OF A NATION

B orn from an ethos of independence and a desire for selfdetermination the United States was an imperfect union despite its idealism. Written in 1777, The Articles of Confederation was a document meant to unite the states in response to the outbreak of The Revolutionary War. Lacking a strong central government, the ability to collect taxes or to conduct the business of the country without the approval of a supermajority of the states. it was a stop gap document.

After independence from England was won The US Constitution would become the nation's founding document. Debates raged over the power of a central government. Federalists insisted that an empowered executive office was necessary. Anti-Federalists argued that this would simply be replacing the deposed King George with a local facsimile. As a compromise the Bill of Rights was established.

OLIVER ELLSWORTH

Arguably, bringing forth our constitution as a federal democracy would not have been possible without the dedication of Oliver Ellsworth. He was born in Connecticut and educated at the College of New Jersey, (which became Princeton). Many of our Founding Fathers attended and became bonded there. Ellsworth was recognized as brilliant, insightful, and independent. He served in the Continental Congress.

In the Constitutional Convention, The Committee of the Whole served as a clearinghouse for ideas that would be incorporated into our Constitution. Ellsworth was a member of the Committee of Detail. This group was tasked with the actual writing of the Constitution. Washington and Franklin chose this group with particular care.

Franklin's most trusted associate, John Rutledge, who was also a Freemason, became the Chairman. Washington's most trusted associate was his aide de camp, Edmund Randolph, another Freemason. Nathaniel Gorham was President of the Continental Congress as the Convention began and was serving as the President of the Committee of the Whole. Ellsworth and James Wilson were intellectuals who understood constitutions and were personally detached from major positions or alliances.

During the ratification process of our constitution, Ellsworth realized that having slavery as a Federal Issue, would ultimately destroy our chances for a federal republic. He felt that remaining a loose confederation of states would leave the country vulnerable to foreign attacks and intervention. This imperative was born out by the War of 19812 some decades later.

The five states from New England had already abolished slavery. Three Southern States would not join America if slavery were abolished in our constitution. Ellsworth personally took a stance with Georgia and the Carolinas that he would support them on states' rights regarding slavery.

Slavery was an irresolvable issue. There would have been no chance for the colonies to unite as a Federal Republic if there was not a compromise on slavery as a federal issue. Ellsworth took a stance for slavery being a states' rights issue. He was well aware that if the states were not united they would not be able to survive any future conflicts and attacks from England or others.

He kept his word to these southern states and the Constitution was ratified. The states being a united, federal democracy enabled our country to withstand the attacks of the War of 1812. Were the United States not fully united, victory would have unlikely, if not impossible.

Ellsworth left the convention immediately after making his stance. He, personally, was clearly against slavery. This was a make or break issue for our Republic. Our federal system was created and established, but the issues regarding slavery remained unresolved. In fact, the issues became heightened.

> *"There were 700 thousand slaves in the US in 1790, which equated to approximately 18 percent of the total population, or roughly one in every six people. By 1860, the final census taken before the American Civil War, there were four million slaves in the South, compared with less than 0.5 million free African Americans in all of the US. Of the 4.4 million African Americans in the US before the war, almost four million of these people were held as slaves; meaning that for all African Americans living in the US in 1860, there was an 89 percent* chance that they lived in slavery.(Statista)*

The other constitutional issue regarding slavery is the three-fifths compromise that was in the Constitution. Northern states did not want slaves to be counted. Southern states wanted all slaves to be counted.

This determination was used to determine taxation as well as the number of delegates in the House of Representatives. Voting was not even a consideration. In other words, Southerners wanted slaves to be counted on issues benefiting population. However, regarding voting and governance, they did not want slaves to be counted whatsoever. Any consideration of suffrage would be an outrage.

Voting Rights

Voting rights was another unresolved issue as our country began. In the Declaration of Independence, Thomas Jefferson wrote, "Governments are instituted among Men, deriving their just Powers from the Consent of the Governed.". The Constitution largely left the question of who was eligible to vote up to the individual states. The founders believed there needed to be a balance. There was the ideal that "all men are created equal" but if everyone was eligible to vote the preeminent position of the landed gentry could be usurped.

New Jersey began with suffrage for women. These rights were eliminated by 1807. In some Northern state free Black men were eligible to vote. In most states, voting was restricted to land owning or tax paying men. It should come as no surprise that the men who wrote the laws and made the rules did so in a way that protected their political power.

Our first six presidents indicated the influence of all prior governing and religious systems The Adams both came from well-educated Puritan lineage. John Quincy Adams had a diplomatic career in Europe dealing with the top tier Monarchs and the Catholic Church hierarchy. The other four were slave owning Virginians also with Anglican heritage. The imbalance of the electoral college giving slave states a greater voice than their actual number of voters was certainly a factor.

As the 7th president, Andrew Jackson presented himself as a "champion of the common man" populist. He railed against special privilege and amassed 70 percent of the electoral college votes in 1828. During his time in office most states changed their voting laws to include all white men. It was another example of those making voting laws that would perpetuate political power.

Population

The African slave trade was abolished in 1807 but the practice continued illegally until the Civil War. Some Southern legislators voted with their Northern counterparts to enact this law. They felt the slave population was self-sustaining and a continued influx would result in whites being outnumbered.

Abolitionists, Quakers who were teaching blacks to be literate, missionaries and others were pushing their agendas. Meanwhile, the slave owners would lose their plurality were the blacks and women given voting rights. White men, who did not own property, were also a threat. These educated founders, who owned property felt their responsibility for ownership and paying taxes enabled them to make the best governmental decisions. Property ownership had always been considered the strongest qualifier for leadership and they were not interested in changing that principle. They had established the first federal democracy.

Social issues increasingly became sourced by lower ranks in society. This began with inclusion of soldiers who fought in the Revolutionary War.

As our democracy took hold, concurrently the Industrial Revolution advanced. This phenomenon had a vastly different impact on the Northern and Southern states in the first half of the 19th century. In the South there where technological advancements. The cotton gin for example made the harvesting of cotton much more efficient and lead to the US supplying 2/3 of the world's supply of cotton. Satisfied with this advancement and handsome profits, the South remained largely agrarian and powered by inexpensive slave labor.

As the Industrial Revolution began in England, the traditional aristocratic leadership created great tension between the classes. Rather than deal with the oppressive class system, they emigrated to America.

In the North, technology and factories shifted manufacturing into high gear. Cheap labor was satisfied by immigrants from Europe. 7 out of every 8 immigrants during this period settled in Northern, largely urban areas. Factories and railroads were built in abundance.

Financial markets that had already been centered in Northern cities grew exponentially. Industrial output from the North boomed. The vast number of working immigrants made their voice known. The workplace had achieved a somewhat democratic basis, which included labor unions. This led to greater participation and interest in governance. Property ownership expanded to the lower ranks. The momentum for voting rights for all had begun.

Agriculture output in the North also outpaced that of the South. Farming became mechanized and vastly more efficient.

Meanwhile, in the south, the slave labor continued to be the engine. It was a labor- intensive, agriculture based economy. It took six slaves to produce the comparable work of a machine commonly used in the North. Problems included poor transportation and a small industrial sector.

By the time the Civil War began population in the North swelled to 23 million as compared to a population of 9 million in the states of the Confederacy.

CHAPTER 16 | INTENSIFING THE DIVISIONS

There were three significant political/judicial controversies: the Missouri Compromise, the Fugitive Slave Act, and the Dred Scott Case.

The Missouri Compromise

The territory of Missouri first applied for statehood in 1817. At the time there were 11 slave states and 11 free states. Representative Tallmadge of <u>New York</u> proposed that Missouri be admitted as a free state. The balance of power was at stake and political fighting ensued. In the North there was a growing sentiment that slavery was morally wrong. In the South, the economy and much of the wealthy was largely tied to slavery. In 1820 a compromise was reached. Maine would break away from Massachusetts becoming the 23rd state and Missouri would be admitted as the 24th, albeit a slave state. The territories of the Louisiana Purchase north of Missouri would be later admitted as free states. Once passed, however, this compromise became the basis for escalating law suits, acts, and actions intensifying the slavery issue. John Quincy Adams noted in his diary, "Take it for granted that the present is a mere preamble—a title page to a great, tragic volume."

This map shows the battleground for the issues of States Rights over Federal Rights, which included, but was not limited to slavery.

Similarities to current political divisions in America remain.

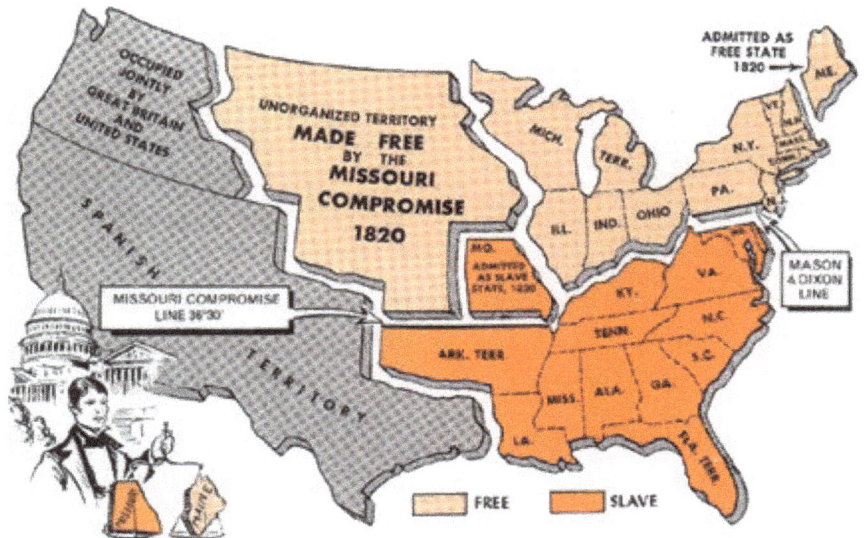

Diagram from (Missouri Compromise)

The Fugitive Slave Act

In 1787 when our Constitution was written the New England States had legally abolished slavery. Southerners strongly felt that slaves would escape to freedom in the North. Northerners felt this was an issue that would be decided over time. With that presumption, they took the risk of including the Fugitive Slave Clause in our Constitution. "Article 4 Section 2 Clause 3" stipulated that a. slave in one state who escapes to a state where slavery is outlawed, will be returned to the slave owner upon their request. In 1793 he first Fugitive Slave Act was passed giving slaveholders greater rights to search for runaway slaves.

Henry Clay wrote the revised Fugitive Act of 1850 as a means to placate the Southern states. It increased the penalties for those not returning fugitive slaves and provided federal commissioners to settle disputes. It was intended to avoid succession, but it heightened the division and was even harder to enforce. Northern states passed laws banning fugitive hunting and Abolitionists became even more impassioned.

The Dred Scott Case

The Dred Scott Case became the iconic judicial focus against slaves. Scott spent years changing his owners and his status as he travelled between free and slave states. He attempted to purchase his freedom from the widow of his slave master in 1843. After being refused he sued for his freedom in Missouri state court. His case eventually went before the Supreme Court with the opinion written by Chief Judge Taney, a dedicated Southerner.

Judge Taney wrote the decision that "all people of African descent, free or enslaved, were not citizens of the United States. They had no rights to sue in Federal Courts. In addition, the Fifth Amendment protected slave owner rights because slaves were their legal property. He also argued the the Missouri Compromise legislation passed was unconstitutional. In other words, Congress had no power or rights to prevent the spread of slavery.

Scott was ultimately freed by the people who knew and loved him through personal channels. However, the outrage against Taney's opinion was intense and wide-spread. This decision was a huge factor as Lincoln began his presidency.

President James Buchanan

As the 15th President Buchanan held office from 1853-61. Greatness, or a lack thereof, is often conferred based on how a leader addresses the challenges he faces. In retirement and after the Civil War had ended Buchanan said, "History will vindicate my memory from every unjust aspersion." Historians consistently ranked him as the worst president ever… until #45 reset the bar.

Buchanan vacillated when leadership was required. In his inaugural address, Buchanan called the territorial issue of slavery "happily, a matter of but little practical importance." There are reports that he influenced the Dred Scott decision. As a Democratic moderate from Pennsylvania, he felt slavery was morally wrong but sided with the South on the issue at every turn. Seen through today's lens he is easily identified as a white supremacist who argued that eliminating slavery would lead to the "introduction of evils infinitely greater." at the expense of "the chivalrous race of men in the South." The country was coming apart at the seams and Buchanan deferred.

Buchanan's successor was elected in November 1860 but would not take office until March 1861. During this four month lame duck period seven Southern states had voted to succeed from the Union. In response, Buchanan stated that he had "no authority to decide what shall be the relation between the federal government and South Carolina." Many in his cabinet resigned in protest.

In a final dereliction of leadership Buchanan wrote:

> *"It is beyond the power of any president, no matter what may be his own political proclivities, to restore peace and harmony among the states. Wisely limited and restrained as is his power under our Constitution and laws, he alone can accomplish but little for good or for evil on such a momentous question."*

Candidate Abraham Lincoln

In 1858, Lincoln challenged incumbent Democrat Stephen Douglas for his US Senate seat in Illinois. In a series of widely publicized debates the two men debated the contentious topic of the day – slavery and its extension in the territories. Douglas was the architect of the Kansas-Nebraska Act that overturned the Missouri Compromise and allowed each new state to decide its status regarding slavery.

Lincoln famously kicked off his campaign with the words:

> *"A house divided against itself cannot stand." I believe this government cannot endure, permanently half slave and half free. I do not expect the Union to be dissolved—I do not expect the house to fall—but I do expect it will cease to be divided. It will become all one thing, or all the other. Either the opponents of slavery, will arrest the further spread of it, and place it where the public mind*

shall rest in the belief that it is in course of ultimate extinction; or
its advocates will push it forward, till it shall become alike lawful
in all the states, old as well as new—North as well as South.

In their debates, Douglas argued that the Constitution had been written by white men whose intent was that it to apply only to white men. Lincoln responded that "there is no reason in the world why the negro is not entitled to all the natural rights enumerated in the <u>Declaration of Independence</u>." Lincoln made no pretense that he would interfere with slavery where it already existed, but argued that the <u>Founding Fathers</u>, many of whom were slaveholders, had regarded slavery as a moral evil that must eventually disappear.

Lincoln garnered 53 percent of the vote but gerrymandering and arcane rules allowed the Democratically led Illinois legislature to choose Douglas as the winner. Lincoln had nonetheless put himself on the map nationally. He voiced a position that resonated with Republican voters. He was against the spread of slavery, maintained a tacit white supremacy common for the times and inferred that the institution of slavery was not sustainable without saying he would abolish it.

The Election of 1860

Presidential candidate Abraham Lincoln built upon his strong showing in the Illinois senate race and entered the fray as a middle of the road candidate. Slavery was a hot button subject but Lincoln's views at that point were well known. As a candidate he strategized to "hedge against divisions in the Republican Party" and "say nothing on points where it is probable we shall disagree. His presidential campaign slogan was an innocuous and westward leaning "Vote yourself a farm and horses". His newly formed Republican party supported homesteads on the Western frontier.

The leading member of the Republican party was New York senator William Steward who was decidedly antislavery. He and the other party hopefuls had each alienated major factions of the party. Lincoln positioned himself as the consensus candidate and became the nominee of the party on the third ballot of the convention.

The Southern powered Democratic Party was rife with division.

The first Democratic party Convention could not pick a candidate after

56 ballots. The delegates decided to reconvene the next month. When they met again the divisive issue was slavery and how it would be handled in the Western territories.

Fifty Southerners left the convention. They were led by an extreme pro-slavery William Yancey, "the fire-eater," and the entire Alabama delegation. A majority of Southerners followed. The Democrats split into two separate parties each nominating their own candidate. Stephen Douglas was considered a moderate on the slavery issue using the term "popular sovereignty." He became the candidate of the Northern Democrats.

The Southern Democrats were united on the pro-slavery platform.

John Breckenridge became their candidate. Breckenridge was President Buchanan's vice-president and had his support. This was very important in his carrying Buchanan's state of Pennsylvania. Interestingly, Jefferson Davis, who later became leader of the Confederate States, was offered being the Presidential Candidate for the Southern Democrats, but he declined.

John Bell was the Constitutional Union Candidate. This party was primarily formed by the remnants of two former parties, the Whigs and the Know-Nothings. They simply avoided the slavery issue.

General Sam Houston, a member of the Constitutional Union Party, had had strong support from Texans. However, without wide support, he dropped out of the race in August and strongly advocated a Unified Ticket to oppose Lincoln. Such a ticket did not come forth from the two Democratic groups.

Lincoln went on to win more than all the other candidates

combined. Lincoln won 180 Electoral College votes out of 303. He received 1.8 million votes, which was 1 million more than the runnerup, Breckenridge who received 72 Electoral College votes. Bell garnered 39 electoral votes and Douglas 12. Many of the Southern local or state voting places did not even issue ballots for Lincoln.

The Confederacy

Shortly after Lincoln was elected but before he took office seven states, with South Carolina in the lead, took steps to secede from the United States. Congress proposed several laws to placate the South without enacting any.. The Crittenden Compromise would have included a Constitutional amendment that would have guaranteed slavery forever in the current slave states.

The Confederate States of America was formed on February 8, 1861 headed by Pres. Jefferson Davis and Vice Pres. Alexander Stephens. Succession was ostensibly over states' rights. In his "Cornerstone Speech" shortly after taking office Stephens opined

> *"The Constitution... rested upon the equality of races. This was an error. Our new government is founded upon exactly the opposite idea; its foundations are laid, its corner-stone rests, upon the great truth that the negro is not equal to the white man; that slavery subordination to the superior race is his natural and normal condition. This, our new government, is the first, in the history of the world, based upon this great physical, philosophical, and moral truth."*

CHAPTER 17 | PRESIDENT LINCOLN

P resident Lincoln took office on March 4th. He attempted to allay Southern fears that he would abolish slavery in his inaugural address.

"Apprehension seems to exist among the people of the Southern States that by the accession of a Republican Administration their property and their peace and personal security are to be endangered. There has never been any reasonable cause for such apprehension. Indeed, the most ample evidence to the contrary has all the while existed and been open to their inspection. It is found in nearly all the published speeches of him who now addresses you. I do but quote from one of those speeches when I declare that "I have no purpose, directly or indirectly, to interfere with the institution of slavery in the States where it exists. I believe I have no lawful right to do so, and I have no inclination to do so."

Manned by US troops, Fort Sumter in Charleston Harbor, South Carolina soon became a flashpoint. Also in his inaugural address, Lincoln referenced the impending conflict.

"You can have no conflict, without being yourselves the aggressors."

Confederate authorities soon demanded that Fort Sumter's be evacuated. With the order refused, shots were fired by the Southern army. Lincoln responded by calling on state governors to provide troops in order to fortify the Union's military forces. This triggered Virginia and the remaining slave states to join the Confederacy. Lincoln ordered a blockade of Southern ports and military conflict was soon at hand.

Starting with the Battle of Bull Run in Virginia, losses for the Union army accumulated. A narrative set in that the Union army was not the equal of that of the Confederacy. To Lincoln's dismay and despite the North's huge industrial and population advantages it had the effect of making the Northern military leaders timid and the Southern commanders overconfident. For two years the South maintained a largely defensive posture with General Lee successfully harassing Northern forces. Indecisive action and the lack of an overarching military strategy by Lincoln's generals proved to be a losing hand for the Union.

In addition to an early military disadvantage Lincoln much to contend with. The North was not united in the war effort. Northern Democrats were pressing for peace and the continuance of slavery. There was sentiment among industrial laborers that freed slaves would take their jobs. The threat of border states jumping ship and joining the Confederacy was ever present. Inflation, war profiteering, Democrats gains in the midterm elections and an uneasy threat that England or France might back the Confederacy were among his concerns.

Lincoln felt constrained on slavery by the Constitution which was understood to leave the issue in the jurisdiction of the states as a matter of property rights. Upon close inspection the Constitution only refers euphemistically to slavery or race in general. Lincoln's initial method for resolving the issue was to offer compensation to slave states in exchange for gradual emancipation and abolition. His plan also called for freed slaves to be sent to foreign colonies. There was a lot not to like in his plan and it was not enacted.

"My paramount object in this struggle is to save the Union, and is not either to save or to destroy slavery. If I could save the Union without freeing any slave I would do it, and if I could save it by freeing all the slaves I would do it; and if I could save it by freeing some and leaving others alone I would also do that. What I do about slavery, and the colored race, I do because I believe it helps to save

the Union... I have here stated my purpose according to my view of official duty; and I intend no modification of my oft-expressed personal wish that all men everywhere could be free."

Doris Kearns Goodwin describes Lincoln's epiphany on slavery thusly:

As his army faltered and his cabinet bickered, Lincoln determined that "we must free the slaves or be ourselves subdued." In 1862, he got his chance. While Washington sweltered through the long, hot summer of 1862, Abraham Lincoln made the momentous decision that would define both his presidency and the course of the Civil War.

The great question of what to do about slavery had provoked increasingly bitter debates on Capitol Hill for months. Back in March, Lincoln had asked the legislature to pass a joint resolution providing federal aid to any state willing to adopt a plan for the gradual abolition of slavery; without the approval of the border-state representatives, it went nowhere. Meanwhile, the Republican majority in Congress, freed from the domination of the Southern bloc, began to push its own agenda on slavery.

Within the cabinet, too, the rancor over slavery infected every discourse. The debates had grown "so bitter," according to Secretary of State William Henry Seward, that personal and even official relationships among members were ruptured, leading to "a prolonged discontinuance of Cabinet meetings." Though Tuesdays and Fridays were still designated for cabinet sessions, each secretary remained in his department unless a messenger arrived to confirm that a meeting would be held. Seward recalled that when these general discussions were still taking place, Lincoln had listened intently but had not taken "an active part in them." For Lincoln, the problem of slavery was not an abstract issue. While he concurred with the most passionate abolitionists that slavery was "a moral, a social and a political wrong," as president, he felt he could not ignore the constitutional protection of the institution where it already existed.

The Army of the Potomac's devastating reverses in the Peninsula Campaign that June made it clear that extraordinary means were necessary to save the Union—and gave Lincoln an opening to deal more directly with slavery.

Daily reports from the battlefields illuminated the innumerable uses to which slaves were put by the Confederacy. They dug trenches and built fortifications for the army. They were brought into camps to serve as teamsters, cooks and hospital attendants, so that soldiers were freed to fight. They labored on the home front, tilling fields, raising crops and picking cotton, so their masters could go to war without fearing that their families would go hungry. If the Rebels were divested of their slaves, who would then be free to join the Union forces, the North could gain a decided advantage. Seen in this light, emancipation could be considered a military necessity—a legitimate exercise of the president's constitutional war powers. A historic decision was taking shape in Lincoln's mind.

The Emancipation Proclamation

Abraham Lincoln signed the Emancipation Proclamation on January 1, 1863 under the guise of his war powers as Commander in Chief. Congress had passed a First Confiscation Act which allowed Union troops to seize rebels' property, including slaves who fought with or worked for the Confederate military. Lincoln's proclamation declared "that all persons held as slaves" within the rebellious states "are, and henceforward shall be free." The emancipation did not apply to the 200,000 slaves held in states that were loyal to the Union. Upon making his proclamation Lincoln remarked:

"I never in my life felt more certain that I was doing right than I do in signing this paper. If my name goes into history, it will be for this act, and my whole soul is in it."

The Emancipation Proclamation did serve to galvanize moral justification for the war. It gave incentive for slaves to escape. It robbed the Confederate war machine of manpower and allowed for Black men to enlist in the Union army.

By the end of the war 200,000 Black men served. Their regiments were largely segregated, often relegated to more mundane tasks such as guard duty or construction. Given the opportunity to battle the Black regiments, performed heroically. Twenty-five Black soldiers were awarded the Medal of Honor for their bravery during the war.

Turning the Tide of War

In the spring of 1863, Robert E Lee went on the offensive. He scored a major victory over the Union Army of the Potomac at Chancellorsville and decided to follow with an excursion into Pennsylvania. Just as Lincoln feared British and French involvement in the war as well as border states leaving the Union for the Confederacy, Lee strategized that a successful campaign in the North would hasten those developments.

General Meade's dramatic, casualty laden victory over Lee at Gettysburg is seen as the beginning of the end for the Confederacy. Meanwhile, Ulysses S Grant had defeated Southern forces in several battles along the Mississippi River culminating in a decisive victory in the strategic fort at Vicksburg. This caught the attention of Lincoln who would name Grant the general in chief of the Union Army in spring of 1864. Lincoln opined that "all he wanted or had ever wanted was someone who would take the responsibility and act."

"Much is being said about peace; and no man desires peace more ardently than I. Still I am yet unprepared to give up the Union for a peace which, so achieved, could not be of much duration."

CHAPTER 18 | LINCOLN AND HIS PROCLAMATIONS

From Washington's presidency forward, Proclamations were commonly an issue for each state by governors and mayors. The range of viewpoints was vast. There were often pleas for Repentance and Humiliation finalizing with Thanksgiving, as in the case with Adams and Madison. There was no connection to the Fall Harvest as was the case of the Pilgrims. It could be any period of the year.

In Lincoln's first year in office he proposed a National Fast Day on September 22, 1861. Unlike earlier Fast days, this was not followed by a day of Thanksgiving. This was a federal directive for repentance and supplication to be implemented on a state and local level. The messages were fervent and heavy reflecting the deteriorating times. As these examples show, the Proclamations were delivered by elected officials as well as religious leaders.

The following examples were printed in the New York Times regarding the National Fast Day.

PROCLAMATION OF GOV. CURTIN, OF PENNSYLVANIA

In the name and by the authority of the Commonwealth of Pennsylvania, ANDREW G. CURTIN, Governor of said Commonwealth --A PROCLAMATION.

Whereas. The President of the United States of America has, by proclamation, appointed Thursday, the 26th day of September current, as a day of public humiliation, prayer and fasting, to be observed by the people of the United States with religious solemnities, and the offering of fervent supplications to Almighty God for the safety and welfare of these States, his blessing on their arms, and a speedy restoration of peace.

Now, therefore, I, ANDREW G. CURTIN, Governor of the Commonwealth of Pennsylvania, do order that on the day named therein the public offices shall be closed, and I earnestly recommend to the people to suspend on that day their ordinary avocations, and to close their places of business, and to humble themselves before the Almighty, with earnest prayers that He will favorably with mercy look upon the people.

Given under my hand and the great seal of State, at Harrisburgh, this nineteenth day of September, in the year of our Lord one thousand eight hundred and sixty-one, (1861,) and of the Commonwealth the eighty-fifth.

PROCLAMATION, By Edwin D. Morgan, Governor of the State of New-York.

The President having recommended the last Thursday in September, instant, as a day of public humiliation, prayer and fasting, to be observed by the people of the United States with religious solemnities and the offering of fervent supplications to Almighty God for the safety and welfare of these States. His blessings on their arms and a speedy restoration of peace, I, EDWIN D. MORGAN, Governor of the State of New-York, in conformity with the proclamation of the President, as well as with my own sense of its propriety, do unite in recommending the people of this State to observe and keep the aforesaid day in all humility, and with all religious solemnity.

Bishop POTTER, of Pennsylvania, has issued an address, recommending the strict observance of the Fast day appointed by the President. He says:

"At no period of our history could such an observance be more proper. Our greatest sin is forgetfulness of God; our greatest peril presumptuous trust in our own wisdom and might. Institutions in which we exulted with impious confidence are in jeopardy; a Union which we boasted that nothing could destroy totters to its fall; material resources with which we thought to defy the world take to themselves wings and fly away. Our reliance on the God of Nations and of Battles needs to be revived and strengthened; and where can this be done but at the footstool of the Divine Mercy? Let us, then, brethren, hasten to the throne of the Heavenly Grace in our closets, in our families and in the sanctuary, and implore of God that He do not forget or forsake us in this our sin, but that He bring us to repentance and a better mind. And on this day, set apart by the highest civil authority, let us assemble in our respective places of worship, and pour out our hearts before the Lord."

In 1862 Lincoln used the term "Thanksgiving Day" for his Proclamation. The theme was still focused on the struggles and humility. Very little of this Announcement attests to Thanksgiving. It embodies a long list of heaviest sorrows.

THANKSGIVING DAY; SEVENTEEN STATES TO OBSERVE THE DAY

November 17, 1862

To-day will be observed as a season of thanksgiving in the following states.. New York, Rhode Island, Connecticut, Pennsylvania, Indiana, Wisconsin, New Jersey, South Carolina, Missouri, Maryland, Maine, Minnesota, Ohio, Massachusetts, Iowa, Illinois, New Hampshire, Kentucky.

In South Carolina the observance of the day will not be general, for Gov. Pickens so far as we are at present informed has not united Go Saxton, in issuing a proclamation. In Vermont Dec 4 has been named as Thanksgiving Day.

We append the proclamations of Go Morgan of the State of New York.

From the depths of national affliction we come, with stricked hearts chastened spirits, to own our dependence upon the Most High, and to render with grateful sense, our thanksgiving for His mercies, countless in number and infinite in extent. A year fraught with the heaviest sorrors has yet, in the merciful plan of Providence, then distinguished by the most conspicuous blessings. Although it is numbered among the dark periods of history and its sorrowful records are graven hearth-stones, yet the precious blood shed in the cause of our country will hallow and strengthen our love and our reverence for it and its institutions. While the bitter sorrows of the year will discipline us into humility. Whatever was passionate in early period of the year, has given way to a deep and subdued conviction of duty into defending the integrity Union. Reflection has made clear our obligation and issues of the monumenous struggles that sells in definite form. Our National aims have been elevated and are our sacrifices have made us less selfish; Our Government and institutions placed in jeopardy have brought us to a more just appreciation of their value.

Looking beyond the wicked leaders, who have participated in this terrible calamity of civil war upon us, we see that the people in arms against the government the higher qualities of our National character; and through their minds have been perverted by passion and prejudice. Yet on many occasion their prowess and devotion to their cause. has been such as to win our respect. We are permitted to see that the war is developing the manhood of the nation; and when peace shall return, we have faith that the American Republic will be more powerful, the government permanent, elements of society, more perfectly blended and the people more firmly united than ever. We have other causes for gratitude. Disease has been everted at home, Unacclimated armies have been protected from pestilence, which it was feared, would follow them in distant latitudes, Earth's best fruits have been lavishly bestowed, the arts have prospered the emplyments of peace have been rewarded, and the good order of society has been fully maintained. Reverses to our arms have followed by successes on land and sea which specially call for thanksgiving and justify the most sanguine expectations as to the final result of the context.

A. Lincoln

The Proclamations were often in the form of Broadsides such as the one following.

These broadsides were written by the local authority and, then, seconded by the President.

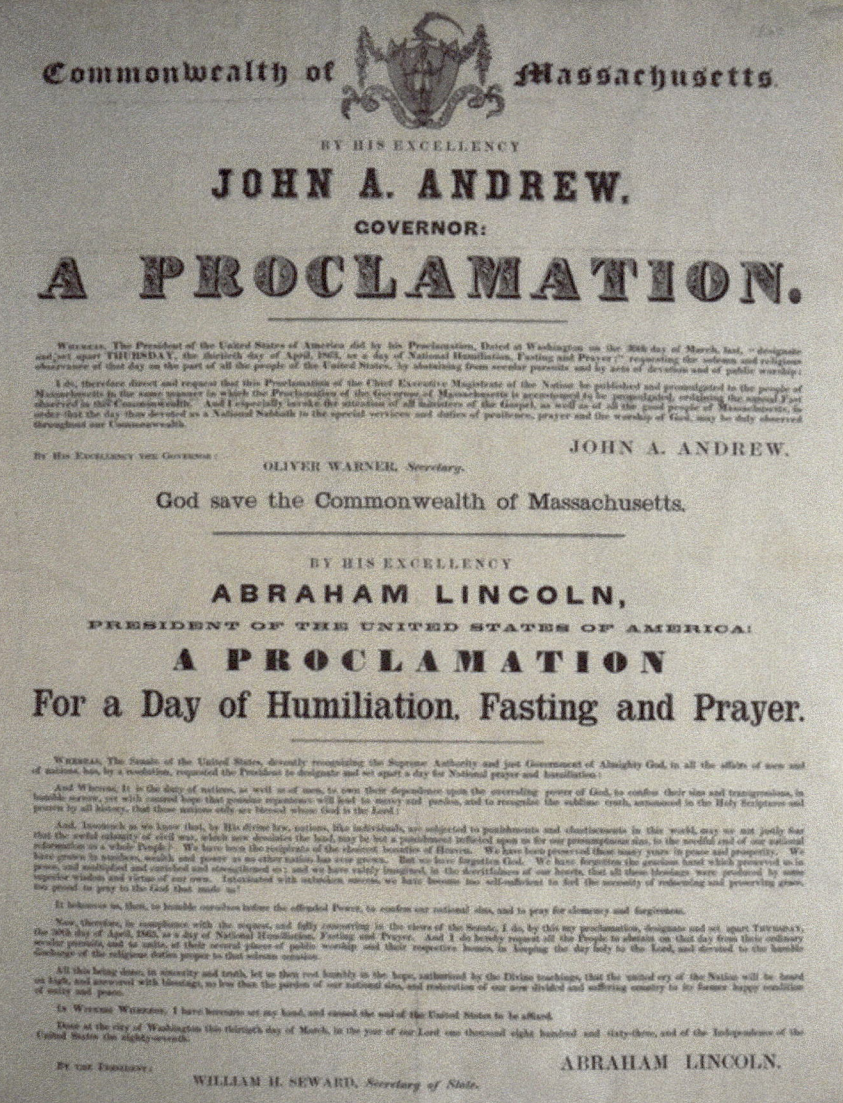

This Broadside was from Governor John Andrew of
Massachusetts and seconded by President Lincoln

As an indication of the depressing feelings of this time, this is the
sole known Broadside in existence.

The proclamation was issued on March 30, 1863 and declared

April 30, 1863 the national day of fasting. This may well have the last National Fast Day. Nowadays such an event would be seen as a violation of the separation of church and state.

It is hard in our times to understand how ingrained Fast Days were in our early Republic. Thanksgiving was not a harvest festival as it had been for the Pilgrims. Fast Days with Religious expression of humiliation were taken seriously. Fast were deliberately humble with the hope that God would save them.

CHAPTER 19 | SARAH JOSEPHA HALE, ADVOCATE

S arah Josepha Duell Hale was born in New Hampshire in 1788 just as our constitution was being ratified. Her father was a Revolutionary War Soldier. Her mother was a well-educated woman, specializing in history and literature. Her older brother, Horatio, went to Dartmouth. From infancy she was part of this dynamic family at a dynamic time. When she was eighteen, she started her own school for girls. In 1813, she married David Hale, who encouraged her literary pursuits. They had five children before he died nine years later.

In 1823, with the support of David Hale's Freemason contacts, she published a book of poems called *The Genius of Oblivion.*, *(Lewis, Jones Johnson)* She immediately went on to publish Poems for Our Children aimed at "inculcating moral truths and virtuous sentiments for our families and children". Mary Had A Little Lamb was one of these instantly famous poems. (Blakemore, E,)

Her next endeavor was a novel Northwood, published in 1827. She advocated that slaves be relocated to Liberia rather than continue to toil in the U.S. It showed the negative effects of slavery on both the enslavers and the enslaved. It attracted the attention of an Episcopal minister, the Rev. John Lauris Blake. He hired her as editor of "Ladies' Magazine", aimed at fashionable women.

This led to her highly successful career as an editor, writer and advocate. The range of her advocacy was extensive, always focusing on family values, activities and patriotism.

As new editor in 1827 she began her campaign for a national day of Thanksgiving. She also thought that Thanksgiving was an opportunity that could bring all Americans together at a time of increasing polarization and sectionalism.

She published articles and wrote letters to presidents and other politicians, religious leaders and national figures. After decades of being dismissed and ridiculed, she hit her mark. In 1863 she wrote to President Lincoln and he immediately took on her work as his policy.

Sarah Hale's Letter to President Lincoln

Philadelphia, Sept. 28th 1863.

Sir,--

Permit me, as Editress of the "Lady's Book", to request a few minutes of your precious time, while laying before you a subject of deep interest to myself and -- as I trust -- even to the President of our Republic, of some importance. This subject is to have the day of our annual Thanksgiving made a National and fixed Union Festival.

You may have observed that, for some years past, there has been an increasing interest felt in our land to have the Thanksgiving held on the same day, in all the States; it now needs National recognition and authoritative fixation, only, to become permanently, an American custom and institution.

Enclosed are three papers (being printed these are easily read) which will make the idea and its progress clear and show also the popularity of the plan.

For the last fifteen years I have set forth this idea in the "Lady's Book", and placed the papers before the Governors of all the States and Territories -- also I have sent these to our Ministers abroad, and our Missionaries to the heathen -- and commanders in the Navy. From the recipients I have received, uniformly the most kind approval. Two of these letters, one from Governor (now General) Banks and one from Governor Morgan are enclosed; both gentlemen as you will see, have nobly aided to bring about the desired Thanksgiving Union.

But I find there are obstacles not possible to be overcome without legislative aid -- that each State should, by statute, make it obligatory on the Governor to appoint the last Thursday of November, annually, as Thanksgiving Day; -- or, as this way would require years to be realized, it has occurred to me that a proclamation from the President of the United States would be the best, surest and most fitting method of National appointment.

I have written to my friend, Hon. Wm. H. Seward, and requested him to confer with President Lincoln on this subject As the President of the United States has the power of appointments for the District of Columbia and the Territories; also for the Army and Navy and all American citizens abroad who claim protection from the U. S. Flag -- could he not, with right as well as duty, issue his proclamation for a Day of National Thanksgiving for all the above classes of persons? And would it not be fitting and patriotic for him to appeal to the Governors of all the States, inviting and commending these to unite in issuing proclamations for the last Thursday in November as the Day of Thanksgiving for the people of each State? Thus the great Union Festival of America would be established.

Now the purpose of this letter is to entreat President Lincoln to put forth his Proclamation, appointing the last Thursday in November (which falls this year on the 26th) as the National Thanksgiving for all those classes of people who are under the National Government particularly, and commending this Union Thanksgiving to each State Executive: thus, by the noble example and action of the President of the United States, the permanency and unity of our Great American Festival of Thanksgiving would be forever secured.

An immediate proclamation would be necessary, so as to reach all the States in season for State appointments, also to anticipate the early appointments by Governors.

Sarah J. Hale

Editress of the "Ladys Book"

CHAPTER 20 | PROCLAMATION OF THANKSGIVING

"I would save the Union. I would save it the shortest way under the Constitution. The sooner the national authority can be restored; the nearer the Union will be the Union as it was." Lincoln

Lincoln's primary focus and self-mandated responsibility had always been to preserve the Union. With the Civil War swinging to the North's favor, Lincoln looked ahead to a once again united United States of America. Bringing the successionist states back into the fold would be no small feat. Sarah Hale's letter was an epiphany moment for Lincoln. Her letter targeted exactly the message he desired, namely Thanksgiving and Unity without any connection whatsoever to Humiliation, Separation and Judgment. Her idea was radical.

Hale wrote her letter on September 28, 1863 and Lincoln took immediate action. Though still emmeshed in a brutal and bloody war, the tenor of this Proclamation was 180 degrees different from his previous bleak and dire missives. Penned by Lincoln's Secretary of State, this iteration is a harbinger of a bright and prosperous future.

Following this Thanksgiving Proclamation but only days before its celebration, Lincoln gave his Gettysburg Address. The themes of "a new birth of freedom," as well as the all-important preservation of the Union were prevalent in both texts.

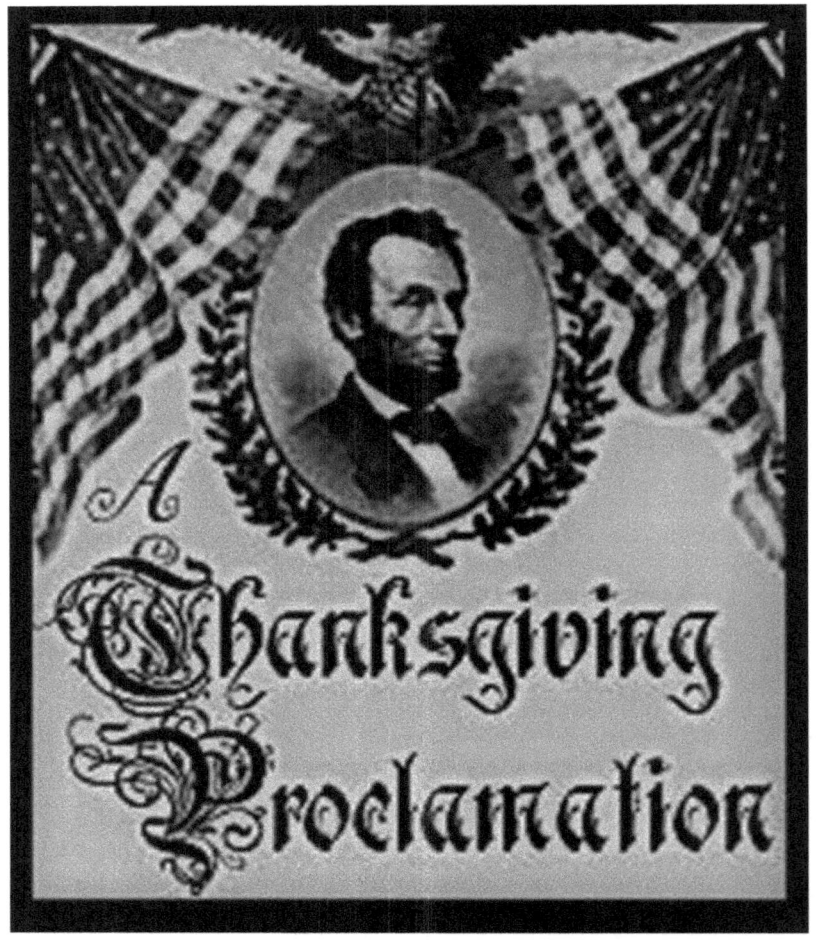

By the President of the United States of America. A Proclamation.

The year that is drawing towards its close, has been filled with the blessings of fruitful fields and healthful skies. To these bounties, which are so constantly enjoyed that we are prone to forget the source from which they come, others have been added, which are of so extraordinary a nature, that they cannot fail to penetrate and soften even the heart which is habitually insensible to the ever watchful providence of Almighty God. In the midst of a civil war of unequalled magnitude and severity, which has sometimes seemed to foreign States to invite and to provoke their aggression, peace has been preserved with all nations, order has been maintained, the laws have been respected and obeyed, and harmony has prevailed everywhere except in the theatre of military conflict; while that theatre has been greatly contracted by the advancing armies and navies of the Union. Needful diversions of wealth and of strength from the fields of peaceful industry to the national defence, have not arrested the plough, the shuttle or the ship; the axe has enlarged the borders of our settlements, and the mines, as well of iron and coal as of the precious metals, have yielded even more abundantly than heretofore. Population has steadily increased, notwithstanding the waste that has been made in the camp, the siege and the battle-field; and the country, rejoicing in the consciousness of augmented strength and vigor, is permitted to expect continuance of years with large increase of freedom. No human counsel hath devised nor hath any mortal hand worked out these great things. They are the gracious gifts of the Most High God, who, while dealing with us in anger for our sins, hath nevertheless remembered mercy. It has seemed to me fit and proper that they should be solemnly, reverently and gratefully acknowledged as with one heart and one voice by the whole American People. I do therefore invite my fellow citizens in every part of the United States, and also those who are at sea and those who are sojourning in foreign lands, to set apart and observe the last Thursday of November next, as a day of Thanksgiving and Praise to our beneficent Father who dwelleth in the Heavens. And I recommend to them that while offering up the ascriptions justly due to Him for such singular deliverances and blessings, they do also, with humble penitence for our national perverseness and disobedience, commend to His tender care all those who have become widows, orphans, mourners or sufferers in the lamentable civil strife in which we are unavoidably engaged, and fervently implore the interposition of the Almighty Hand to heal the wounds of the nation and to restore it as soon as may be consistent with the Divine purposes to the full enjoyment of peace, harmony, tranquillity and Union. In testimony whereof, I have hereunto set my hand and caused the Seal of the United States to be affixed. Done at the City of Washington, this Third day of October, in the year of our Lord one thousand eight hundred and sixty-three, and of the Independence of the United States the Eighty-eighth. By the President: Abraham Lincoln

A. Lincoln

Lincoln followed his first Proclamation with another in 1864 establishing a tradition. We have had a Thanksgiving Proclamation every year thereafter.

Thanksgiving Proclamation
October 20, 1864
by the President of the United States of America

a Proclamation

It has pleased Almighty God to prolong our national life another year, defending us with His guardian care against unfriendly designs from abroad and vouchsafing to us in His mercy many and signal victories over the enemy, who is of our own household. It has also pleased our Heavenly Father to favor as well our citizens in their homes as our soldiers in their camps and our sailors on the rivers and seas with unusual health. He has largely augmented our free population by emancipation and by immigration, while He has opened to us new sources of wealth and has crowned the labor of our workingmen in every department of industry with abundant rewards. Moreover, He has been pleased to animate and inspire our minds and hearts with fortitude, courage, and resolution sufficient for the great trial of civil war into which we have been brought by our adherence as a nation to the cause of freedom and humanity, and to afford to us reasonable hopes of an ultimate and happy deliverance from all our dangers and afflictions:

Now, therefore, I, Abraham Lincoln, President of the United States, do hereby appoint and set apart the last Thursday in November next as a day which I desire to be observed by all my fellow-citizens, wherever they may then be, as a day of thanksgiving and praise to Almighty God, the beneficent Creator and Ruler of the Universe. And I do further recommend to my fellow-citizens aforesaid that on that occasion they do reverently humble themselves in the dust and from thence offer up penitent and fervent prayers and supplications to the Great Disposer of Events for a return of the inestimable blessings of peace, union, and harmony throughout the land which it has pleased Him to assign as a dwelling place for ourselves and for our posterity throughout all generations.

In testimony whereof I have hereunto set my hand and caused the seal of the United States to be affixed.

Done at the city of Washington, this 20th day of October, A.D. 1864, and of the Independence of the United States the eighty-ninth.

ABRAHAM LINCOLN.

Lincoln Postscript

Lincoln died on April 15, 1865 so that this was his last directive for Thanksgiving. He established an annual National Thanksgiving Proclamation and Event. President Andrew Johnson continued this practice.

Following Lincoln's lead, Thanksgivings have since been apolitical and not religious. Fasting, Humiliation and Repentance permanently omitted. It has elements of a harvest festival, it is a bonding time for families and more recently a kick-off for holiday shopping. Increasingly there are cross-cultural practices including religions. Our annual national celebrations are The Fourth of July celebrating our constitution and the birth of our Nation and Thanksgiving celebrating our core values as Americans.

Sarah Hale lived to be 89. She advocated for women's education and employment helping to found Vassar College. Widely published in books and magazines, Hale was recognized as a tastemaker for

American women. She also promoted physical education as vital to children's education.

> *"Physical health and its attendant cheerfulness promote a happy tone of moral feeling, and they are quite indispensable to successful intellectual effort.*

Civil War postscript

After several failed attempts, on January 31, 1865, the House of Representatives addressed the holes in the Emancipation Proclamation by passing the 13th Amendment with a vote of 119-56, just over the required two-thirds majority. The following day, Lincoln approved a joint resolution of Congress submitting it to the state legislatures for ratification. The 13th Amendment states:

> *"Neither slavery nor involuntary servitude, except as a punishment for crime whereof the party shall have been duly convicted, shall exist within the United States, nor any place subject to their jurisdiction."*

The 14th Amendment, passed by Congress in 1866 and ratified in 1868, granted citizenship to all persons born or naturalized in the United States—including former enslaved people—and guaranteed all citizens "equal protection of the laws."

These Amendments were giant steps forward but did not cure all the blind spots in the Constitution. Lincoln did not live to see final ratification of either Amendment.

CHAPTER 21 | OUR THANKSGIVING TRADITION

Arguably, the three most important events in shaping the United States of America also directly led to our Thanksgiving tradition. Success in all three of these events was far from assured and at times unlikely. A different outcome in any three would have resulted in a place remarkably different than the one we now take for granted. Celebrations as called for by Presidents Washington and Lincoln followed a period of great division.

From its roots, Thanksgiving is a celebration of gratitude, unity and survival. There are a myriad of problematic issues as seen through today's lens with the colonization of North America. Consequences for the native population were absolutely devastating. As seen on a micro level, the survival of the Pilgrims as aided by the Wampanoag and the peace treaty proposed by Massasoit was about cooperation.

Having this specific group of people as the first to colonize New England reverberates through history. A congregation seeking a place to avoid religious persecution combined with merchant adventurers who were not specifically concerned with religion was critical. The Mayflower Compact as agreed upon by both groups established a separation of church and state. It also codified a classless system of government with "just and equal laws". Descendants of this small group have made their mark through history.

Victory in the American Revolution and the founding of the United

States was monumental. Throwing off the yoke of British sovereignty was the first step to creating our form of self-government. Based on the ideals of the Declaration of Independence and codified by The Constitution and Bill of Rights this new nation was designed to be a fair and just nation of laws. The ideal of all men being equal was expressed, if not exactly put into action.

This group of people, as led by the Founding Fathers, set out on their "great experiment" to create a nation committed to the ideals of life, liberty and the pursuit of happiness. There were different ideas of how this should be accomplished but the goal was shared.

Perhaps the greatest trait among them, most notably Washington, was that none put himself before the country. All acted knowing full well that the eyes of history would forever be on them. A collective well-being was the objective. Having all 13 colonies united in common because was seen as the key to the fledging Republic's stability, success and survival.

President Washington's Thanksgiving Proclamation was expressly a celebration of a new nation and a brighter future.

President Lincoln faced the herculean task of reuniting a severely fractured United States. Divisions and injustices that were not properly addressed in the Constitution festered reaching a boiling point just as he was to take office. In the bloodiest of all American wars, Lincoln sought to preserve the Union. He took bold steps to advance civil liberties for all. In an effort to heal a divided nation he issued his Thanksgiving Proclamation and established our enduring Thanksgiving tradition.

Since Lincoln, Thanksgiving Proclamations have been a tradition for every President, every year.

CHAPTER 22 | MAYFLOWER CONNECTIONS TO SOME OF OUR PRESIDENTS

A Mayflower Story: The voyage across the Atlantic was tumultuous. There were cramped quarters, raging storms and the trip was very long. John Howland, an indentured servant, went up on the deck during a brief lull and was swept overboard. In the annals of miracles, this one ranks supreme. He caught a rope and was saved. In fact, he was the longest living passenger from the list.

His descendants include FDR, George Bush #41 and George Bush #43. Howland's brothers, Henry II and Arthur, immigrated soon thereafter.

Henry Howland was the ancestor of Richard Nixon and Gerald Ford. Arthur Howland was an ancestor of Winston Churchill. It is impossible to think of the 20th Century without recognition of that miracle.

Mayflower ancestors of US Presidents

President John Adams #2 and his son, John Quincy Adams #6, were descendants of John and Priscilla (Mullins) Alden, and William Mullins; John Adams gave a proclamation for repentance.

JQA did not give a proclamation.

President Zachary Taylor (1784-1850), #12 President, descendant of Isaac Allerton, and William and Mary Brewster. He did not give a Proclamation.

President Ulysses S. Grant, #18, descendant of Richard and Elizabeth (Walker) Warren; Grant gave a proclamation.

James A. Garfield, #20, descendant of John and Elinor Bollington, and Francis Bollington; Since Garfield was assassinated and died after only 200 days in office, he sadly never gave his proclamations.

Calvin Coolidge, #30, descendant of Edward Doty.

Franklin D. Roosevelt (1882-1945), 32nd President, descendant of Isaac Allerton, Francis Cooke, John and Elizabeth (Tilley) Howland, Decory Priest, John and Joan (Hurst) Tilley, and Richard and Elizabeth (Walker) Warren.

George H. W. Bush #31 President, descendant of John and Elizabeth (Tilley) Howland, Francis Cooke, and John and Joan (Hurst) Tilley;

George W. Bush #33 descendant of John and Elizabeth (Tilley) Howland, Francis Cooke, and John and Joan (Hurst) Tilley; Henry Samson. His mother, Barbara Bush was also a Mayflower descendant.

Three descended from the Mayflower Colonists - First Generation

Descendants of Henry Howland Jr
Richard Nixon (1969 to 1974) 37th
Gerald Ford (1974 to 1977) 38th

The Mayflower was followed by The Fortune (1621), The Anne (1623), and The Little James (1623). The Fortune arrived in December 1621, after the first Thanksgiving. Passengers on these four boats were called the "First Comers."

Descendant of Speedwell Ancestor Thomas Blossom: Barack Obama
The direct ancestors of Barack Obama #44, Thomas and Anne Blossom were passengers on the Speedwell, the leaky sister ship of the Mayflower that had to be abandoned. The Blossoms chose to return to Holland and embark later. After the death of Pastor John

Robinson in 1626, Thomas became the spiritual leader of the entire congregation from Leiden.

Pastor Thomas Blossom organized a fleet of six ships, which sailed to Plymouth Colony in 1629. He and his wife, Anne, were on the lead ship, the Mayflower II. He died in the flu epidemic of 1632.

CHAPTER 23 | SELECTED PROCLAMATIONS FROM THE MAYFLOWER & MAYFLOWER COLONY DECENDANTS

ULYSSES S. GRANT #18

Proclamation 217
Thanksgiving Day, October 14, 1873

By the President of the United States of America

The approaching close of another year brings with it the occasion for renewed thanksgiving and acknowledgment to the Almighty Ruler of the Universe for the unnumbered mercies which He has bestowed upon us.

Abundant harvests have been among the rewards of industry. With local exceptions, health has been among the many blessings enjoyed. Tranquility at home and peace with other nations have prevailed.

Frugal industry is regaining its merited recognition and its merited rewards.

Gradually but, under the providence of God, surely, as we trust, the nation is recovering from the lingering results of a dreadful civil strife.

For these and all the other mercies vouchsafed it becomes us as a people to return heartfelt and grateful acknowledgments, and with our thanksgiving for blessings we may unite prayers for the cessation of local and temporary sufferings.

I therefore recommend that on Thursday, the 27th day of November next, the people meet in their respective places of worship to make their acknowledgments to Almighty God for His bounties and His protection, and to offer to Him prayers for their continuance.

In witness whereof I have hereunto set my hand and caused the seal of the United States to be affixed.

Done at the city of Washington, this 14th day of October, A.D. 1873, and of the Independence of the United States the ninety-eighth. U.S. GRANT

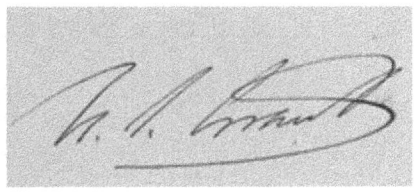

CALVIN COOLIDGE, #30

November 05, 1924

By the President of the United States of America

We approach that season of the year when it has been the custom for the American people to give thanks for the good fortune which the bounty of Providence, through the generosity of nature, has visited upon them. It is altogether a good custom. It has the sanction of antiquity and the approbation of our religious convictions. In acknowledging the receipt of divine favor, in contemplating the blessings which have been bestowed upon us, we shall reveal the spiritual strength of the nation.

I therefore recommend that on Thursday, the 27th day of November next, the people meet in their respective places of worship to make their acknowledgments to Almighty God for His bounties and His protection, and to offer to Him prayers for their continuance. In witness whereof I have hereunto set my hand and caused the seal of the United States to be affixed. Done at the city of Washington, this 14th day of

October, A.D. 1873, and of the Independence of the United States the ninety-eighth. Have been bountiful. We have been remarkably free from disorder and remarkably successful in all those pursuits which flourish during a state of domestic peace. An abundant prosperity has overspread the land. We shall do well to accept all these favors and bounties with a becoming humility, and dedicate them to the service of the righteous cause of the Giver of all good and perfect gifts. As the nation has prospered let all the people show that they are worthy to prosper by rededicating America to the service of God and man.

Therefore, I, Calvin Coolidge, President of the United States of America, hereby proclaim and fix Thursday, the twenty-seventh day of November, as a day of National thanksgiving. I recommend that the people gather in their places of worship, and at the family altars, and offer up their thanks for the goodness which has been shown to them in such a multitude of ways. Especially I urge them to supplicate the Throne of Grace that they may gather strength from their tribulations, that they may gain humility from their victories, that they may bear without complaining the burdens that shall be placed upon them, and that they may be increasingly worthy in all ways of the blessings that shall come to them. In Witness Whereof, I have hereunto set my hand and caused the seal of the United States to be done at the City of Washington., this fifth day of November, in the year of our Lord, one thousand nine hundred and twenty-four, and of the independence of the United States the one hundred and forty-ninth.

CALVIN COOLIDGE

FRANKLIN DELANO ROOSEVELT #32

FDR's first Thanksgiving Proclamation *at the height of the Great Depression*

A Proclamation

I, Franklin D. Roosevelt, President of the United States of America, do set aside and appoint Thursday, the thirtieth day of November, 1933, to be a Day of Thanksgiving for all our people.

May we on that day in our churches and in our homes give humble thanks for the blessings bestowed upon us during the year past by Almighty God. May we recall the courage of those who settled a wilderness, the vision of those who founded the Nation, the steadfastness of those who in every succeeding generation have fought to keep pure the ideal of equality of opportunity and hold clear the goal of mutual help in time of prosperity as in time of adversity? May we ask guidance in more surely learning the ancient truth that greed and selfishness and striving for undue riches can never bring lasting happiness or good to the individual or to his neighbors? May we be grateful for the passing of dark days; for the new spirit of dependence one on another; for the closer unity of all parts of our wide land; for the greater friendship between employers and those who toil; for a clearer knowledge by all Nations that we seek no conquests and ask only honorable engagements by all peoples to respect the lands and rights of their neighbors; for the brighter day to which we can win through by seeking the help of God in a more unselfish striving for the common bettering of mankind. In Witness Whereof, I have hereunto set my hand and caused the seal of the United States to be affixed.

Franklin D. Roosevelt

FRANKLIN D. ROOSEVELT

Lincoln set Thanksgiving Day as the last Thursday in November. In 1939 FDR made a change. That November included five Thursdays. In an effort to move up what had become the beginning of the Christmas shopping season he moved the date to the next to last Thursday. He repeated this controversial challenge to tradition in 1940 & 1941.

Bowing to public opinion but negating the disadvantage of a five Thursday month, Roosevelt signed a bill into law officially making the fourth Thursday in November the national holiday of Thanksgiving Day.

FDR's 1942 Proclamation was his first as a war time president.

By the President of the United States of America a Proclamation?

"It is a good thing to give thanks unto the Lord." Across the uncertain ways of space and time our hearts echo those words, for the days are with us again when, at the gathering of the harvest, we solemnly express our dependence upon Almighty God.

The final months of this year, now almost spent, find our Republic and the Nations joined with it waging a battle on many fronts for the preservation of liberty.

In giving thanks for the greatest harvest in the history of our Nation, we who plant and reap can well resolve that in the year to come we will do all in our power to pass that milestone; for by our labors in the fields we can share some part of the sacrifice with our brothers and sons who wear the uniform of the United States. It is fitting that we recall now the reverent words of George Washington, "Almighty God, we make our earnest prayer that Thou wilt keep the United States in Thy holy Protection," and that every American in his own way lift his voice to heaven. I recommend that all of us bear in mind this great Psalm: "The Lord is my shepherd; I shall not want. "He market me to lie down in green pastures: he leaded me beside the still waters. "He restored my soul; he leaded me in the paths of righteousness for his name's sake."Yea, though I walk through the valley of the shadow of death, I will fear no evil: for thou art with me; thy rod and thy staff they comfort me. "Thou preparest a table before me in the presence of mine enemies: thou anointest my head with oil; my cup runneth over. "Surely goodness and mercy shall follow me all the days of my life: and I will dwell in the house of the Lord for ever." Inspired with faith and courage by these words, let us turn again to the work that confronts us in this time of national emergency: in the armed services and the merchant marine; in factories and offices; on farms and in the mines; on highways, railways, and airways; in other places of public service to the Nation; and in our homes. Now, Therefore, I, Franklin D. Roosevelt, President of the United States of America, do hereby invite the attention of the people to the joint resolution of Congress approved December 26, 1941, which designates the fourth Thurday in November of each year as Thanksgiving Day, November 26, 1942 and New Years Day, January q, 1943, to be observed in prayer, publicly and privately.

FRANKLIN D. ROOSEVELT

RICHARD NIXON #37

By the President of the United States of America

A Proclamation

One of the splendid events which shapes man's destiny occurred when a small band of people, believing in the essential sanctity of their own being, went in search of a land in which their individuality might be the highest national value, before any arbitrary limitation or duty placed upon some men by the whim or design of others. They went in search of a land where they might live out their own commitment to their own ideal of human freedom. In the purpose of their search, the human spirit found its ultimate definition, and in the product of their search, its ultimate expression. They found the land they sought, and it was a difficult land, but it was rich. With their sacrifices they brought forth its riches, and laid the foundation for a new nation.

But more than that, they revealed a new possibility for the expression of man's spirit. In the sure unfolding of that possibility man has begun to experience a world in which he may do justice, love mercy and walk humbly with his god forever.

For what those early settlers established, we give thanks in a way which began with them. In their first years on the hard cold edge of man's bright golden-dream, they were tried and their faith was tested. But when their bodies failed, their faith did not.

The stark simple words on a sarcophagus in a little village on the seacoast of Massachusetts tell the story well: "This monument marks the first burying-ground in Plymouth of the passengers of the Mayflower. Here, under cover of darkness, the fast dwindling company laid their dead; leveling the earth above them lest the Indians should learn how many were the graves." Yet, because mankind was not created merely to survive, in the fact of all hardship and suffering, these men and women - and those of the other early settlements - prevailed. And the settlers gathered to give thanks for God's bounty, for the blessings of life itself, and for the freedom which they so cherished that no hardship could quench it. And now their heritage is ours. What they dared to imagine for this land came to pass. What they planted here prospered.

And for our heritage - a land rich with the bountiful blessings of God, and the freedom to enjoy those rich blessings - we give thanks to God Almighty in this time, and for all time.

Now, Therefore, I, Richard M. Nixon, President of the United States of America in accordance with the wish of the Congress as expressed in Section 6103 of Title 5 of the United States Code, do hereby proclaim Thursday, November 25, 1971, as a day of national thanksgiving. I call upon all Americans to share this day, to give thanks in homes and in places of worship for the many blessings our people enjoy, to welcome the elderly and less fortunate as special participants in this day's festivities and observances, thereby truly showing our gratitude to God by expressing and reflecting His love.

In Witness Whereof, I have hereunto set my hand this fifth day of November, in the year of our Lord nineteen hundred seventy-one, and of the Independence of the United States of America the one hundred ninety-sixth.

RICHARD NIXON

ERALD R FORD # 38

A Proclamation

Two hundred years ago the frontier colonies of America braced for a long and determined conflict with the strongest military pow er in the world. The petition of our Founding Fathers for redress of their grievances had been rejected by King and Parliament, and the people of America began the struggle from which emerged this great Nation. Our

Nation is the oldest continuously surviving republic in the world. For 200 years our freedoms have been questioned, challenged, tested and reinforced. These freedoms have shaped our destiny and served as a beacon to other peoples. Our Nation draws its strength from people of every creed, of every color, of every race - native Americans and people from every nation in the world who for two centuries have come to share in the rewards and responsibilities of our American Republic. On the eve of our 200th year, Thanksgiving Day should be a day of special reflection upon the qualities of heart, mind and character of the men and women who founded and built our great Nation. Let us join in giving thanks for our cultural pluralism. Let us celebrate our diversity and the great strengths that have come from sharing our traditions, our ideas, our resources, our hopes and our dreams. Let us be grateful that for 200 years our people have been dedicated to fulfilling the democratic ideal - dedicated to securing "liberty and justice for all." Now, Therefore, I, Gerald R. Ford, President of the United States of America, in accord with Section 6103 of Title 5 of share with our senior citizens and with those less fortunate than ourselves this special day that brings us all closer together. In Witness Whereof, I have hereunto set my hand this fourth day of November, in the year of our Lord nineteen hundred seventyfive, and of the Independence of the United States of America the two hundredth.

GERALD R. FORD

GEORGE HERBERT WALKER BUSH #41

THANKSGIVING DAY 1989

BY THE PRESIDENT OF THE UNITED STATES OF AMERICA

On Thanksgiving Day, we Americans pause as a Nation to give thanks for the freedom and prosperity prosperity with which we have been blessed by our Creator. Like the pilgrims who first settled in this land, we offer praise to God for His goodness and generosity and rededicate ourselves to lives of service and virtue in His sight.

This annual observance of Thanksgiving was a cherished American tradition even before our first President, George Washington, issued the first Presidential Thanksgiving proclamation in 1789. In his first Inaugural Address, President Washington observed that "No people can be bound to acknowledge and adore the Invisible Hand which conducts the affairs of men more than those of the United States." He noted that the American people - blessed with victory in their fight for Independence and with an abundance of crops in their fields - owed God "some return of pious gratitude." Later, in a confidential note to his close advisor, James Madison, he asked "should the sense of the Senate be taken on ... a day of Thanksgiving?" George Washington thus led the way to a Joint Resolution of Congress requesting the President to set aside "a day of public Thanksgiving and Prayer, to be observed by acknowledging with grateful hearts the many and signal Favors of Almighty God." Through the eloquent words of President Washington's initial Thanksgiving proclamation - the first under the Constitution - we are reminded of our dependence upon our Heavenly Father and of the debt of gratitude we owe to Him. "It is the Duty of all Nations," wrote Washington, "to acknowledge the Providence of almighty God, to obey his Will, to be grateful for his Benefits, and humbly to implore His Protection and Favor." President Washington asked that on Thanksgiving Day the people of the United States: unite in rendering unto [God] our sincere and humble Thanks for his kind Care and Protection of the People of this Country previous to their becoming a Nation; for ... the great degree of Tranquility, Union and Plenty which we have since enjoyed; for ... the civil and religious Liberty with which we are blessed, and ... for all the great and various Favors which he hath been pleased to confer upon us. Two hundred years later, we continue to offer thanks to the Almighty - not only for the material prosperity that our Nation enjoys, but also for the blessings of peace and freedom. Our Nation has no greater treasures than these. As we pause to acknowledge the kindnesses God has shown to us - and, indeed, His gift of llfe itself - we do so in a spirit of humility as well as gratitude. When the United States was still a fledgling democracy, President Washington asked the American people to unite in prayer to the "great Lord and ruler of Nations," in order to: beseech him to pardon our national and other Transgressions; to enable us all, whether in public or private Stations, to perform our several and relative Duties properly and punctually; to render our national Government a blessing to all the People, by constantly being a Government of wise, just and constitutional Laws, discreetly and faithfully executed and obeyed; to protect and guide all Sovereigns and Nations … and to bless them with good Government, peace and Concord. Today, we, too, pause on Thanksgiving with humble and contrite hearts, mindful of God's mercy and forgiveness and of our continued need for His protection and guidance. On this day, we also remember that one gives praise to God not only through prayers of thanksgiving, but also through obedience to His commandments and service to others, especially those less fortunate than ourselves. While some Presidents followed Washington's precedent, and some State Governors did as well, President Lincoln - despite being faced with the dark specter of civil war - renewed the practice of proclaiming a national day of Thanksgiving. This venerable tradition has been sustained by every President since then, in times of strife as well as times of peace and prosperity. Today, we continue to offer thanks and praise to our Creator, that "Great Author of every public and private good," for the many blessings He has bestowed upon us. In so doing, we recall the timeless words of the 100th Psalm: Serve the Lord with gladness: come before His presence with singing. Know ye that the Lord He is God: it is He that hath made us, and not we ourselves; we are His people, and the sheep of His pasture. Enter into His gates with thanksgiving, and into His courts with praise: be thankful unto Him, and bless His name. For the Lord is good; His mercy is everlasting; and His truth endureth to all generations. Now, Therefore, I, George Bush, President of the United States of America, do hereby proclaim Thursday, November 23, 1989, as a National Day of Thanksgiving, and I call upon the American people to gather together in homes and places of worship on that day of thanks to affirm by their prayers and their gratitude the many blessings God has bestowed upon us and our Nation. In Witness Whereof, I have hereunto set my hand this seventeenth day of November, in the year of our Lord nineteen hundred and eighty-nine, and of the Independence of the United States of America the two hundred and fourteenth.

GEORGE H. W. BUSH

GEORGE WALKER BUSH #43

November 16, 2001

by the President of the United States of America a

Proclamation

Nearly half a century ago, President Dwight Eisenhower proclaimed Thanksgiving as a time when Americans should celebrate "the plentiful yield of our soil . . . the beauty of our land . . . the preservation of those ideals of liberty and justice that form the basis of our national life, and the hope of international peace." Now, in the painful aftermath of the September 11 attacks and in the midst of our resolute war on terrorism, President Eisenhower's hopeful words point us to our collective obligation to defend the enduring principles of freedom that form the foundation of our Republic. During these extraordinary times, we find particular assurance from our Thanksgiving tradition, which reminds us that we, as a people and individually, always have reason to hope and trust in God, despite great adversity. In 1621 in New England, the Pilgrims gave thanks to God, in whom they placed their hope, even though a bitter winter had taken many of their brethren. In the winter of 1777, General George Washington and his army, having just suffered great misfortune, stopped near Valley Forge, Pennsylvania, to give thanks to God. And there, in the throes of great difficulty, they found the hope they needed to persevere. That hope in freedom eventually inspired them to victory. In 1789, President Washington, recollecting the countless blessings for which our new Nation should give thanks, declared the first National Day of Thanksgiving. And decades later, with the Nation embroiled in a bloody civil war, President Abraham Lincoln revived what is now an annual tradition of issuing a presidential proclamation of Thanksgiving. President Lincoln asked God to "heal the wounds of the nation and to restore it as soon as may be consistent with the Divine purposes to the full enjoyment of peace, harmony, tranquility, and Union." unimaginable loss; and let us reach out with care to those in need of food, shelter, and words of hope. May Almighty God, who is our refuge and our strength in this time of trouble, watch over our homeland, protect us, and grant us patience, resolve, and wisdom in all that is to come. Now, Therefore, I, George W. Bush, President of the United States of America, by virtue of the authority vested in me by the Constitution and laws of the United States, do hereby proclaim Thursday, November 22, 2001, as a National Day of Thanksgiving. I encourage Americans to assemble in their homes, places of worship, or community centers to reinforce ties of family and community, express our profound thanks for the many blessings we enjoy, and reach out in true gratitude and friendship to our friends around the world.

In Witness Whereof, I have hereunto set my hand this sixteenth day of November, in the year of our Lord two thousand one, and of the Independence of the United States of America the two hundred and twenty-sixth.

GEORGE W. BUSH

SPEEDWELL AND MAYFLOWER 2 Barack Obama #44

President Barack Obama is a direct descendant of Deacon Thomas Blossom, who became head of this congregation upon the death of John Robinson. Thomas Blossom came in 1629 on Mayflower II,

President Barack Obama, #44
 November 23, 2010
 Presidential Proclamation
 Thanksgiving Day
 A beloved American tradition, Thanksgiving Day offers us the opportunity to focus our thoughts on the grace that has been extended to our people and our country. This spirit brought together the newly arrived Pilgrims and the Wampanoag tribe -- who had been living and thriving around Plymouth, Massachusetts for thousands of years -- in an autumn harvest feast centuries ago. This Thanksgiving Day, we reflect on the compassion and contributions of Native Americans, whose skill in agriculture helped the early colonists survive, and whose rich culture continues to add to our Nation's heritage. We also pause

our normal pursuits on this day and join in a spirit of fellowship and gratitude for the year's bounties and blessings.

Thanksgiving Day is a time each year, dating back to our founding, when we lay aside the troubles and disagreements of the day and bow our heads in humble recognition of the providence bestowed upon our Nation? Amidst the uncertainty of a fledgling experiment in democracy,

President George Washington declared the first Thanksgiving in America, recounting the blessings of tranquility, union, and plenty that shined upon our young country. In the dark days of the Civil War when the fate of our Union was in doubt, President Abraham Lincoln proclaimed a Thanksgiving Day, calling for "the Almighty hand" to heal and restore our Nation.

In confronting the challenges of our day, we must draw strength from the resolve of previous generations who faced their own struggles and take comfort in knowing a brighter day has always dawned on our great land. As we stand at the close of one year and look to the promise of the next, we lift up our hearts in gratitude to God for our many blessings, for one another, and for our Nation. This Thanksgiving Day, we remember that the freedoms and security we enjoy as Americans are protected by the brave men and women of the United States Armed Forces. These patriots are willing to lay down their lives in our defense, and they and their families deserve our profound gratitude for their service and sacrifice.

This harvest season, we are also reminded of those experiencing the pangs of hunger or the hardship of economic insecurity. Let us return the kindness and generosity we have seen throughout the year by helping our fellow citizens weather the storms of our day.

As Americans gather for the time-honored Thanksgiving Day meal, let us rejoice in the abundance that graces our tables, in the simple gifts that mark our days, in the loved ones who enrich our lives, and in the gifts of a gracious God. Let us recall that our forebears met their challenges with hope and an unfailing spirit, and let us resolve to do the same.

NOW, THEREFORE, I, BARACK OBAMA, President of the United States of America, by virtue of the authority vested in me by the Constitution and the laws of the United States, do hereby proclaim Thursday, November 25, 2010, as a National Day of Thanksgiving. I encourage all the people of the United States to come together -- whether in our homes, places of worship, community centers, or any place of fellowship for friends and neighbors -- to give thanks for all we have received in the past year, to express appreciation to those whose lives enrich our own, and to share our bounty with others.

IN WITNESS WHEREOF, I have hereunto set my hand this twenty-third day of November, in the year of our Lord two thousand ten, and of the Independence of the United States of America the two hundred and thirty-fifth.

BARACK OBAMA

MAYFLOWER COLONY DESCENDANT BRITISH PRIME MINISTER SIR WINSTON CHURCHILL

Churchill and FDR were both Mayflower Colony descendants from Henry Howland Sr. Churchill was descendant of John Howland's brother, Arthur. Their strategic alliance was paramount in WWII. Churchill gave a radio address honoring our Thanksgiving after the USA entered WWII

THE THANKSGIVING ADDRESS

We have come here tonight to add our celebration to those which are going forward all over the world wherever Allied troops are fighting, in bivouacs and dug-outs, on battlefields, on the high seas, and in the highest air. Always this annual festival has been dear to the hearts of the American people. Always there has been that desire for thanksgiving, and never, I think, has there been more justification, more compulsive need than now.

It is your Day of Thanksgiving, and when we feel the truth of the facts which are before us, that in three or four years the peaceful peace-loving people of the United States, with all the variety and freedom of their life in such contrast to the iron discipline which has governed many other communities—when we see that in three or four years the United States has in sober fact become the greatest military, naval, and air power in the world—that, I say to you in this time of war, is itself a subject for profound thanksgiving. we are moving forward in this struggle which spreads over all the lands and all the oceans. We are moving forward surely, steadily, irresistibly, and perhaps, with God's aid, swiftly, towards victorious peace. There again is a fitting reason for thanksgiving.

I have spoken of American Thanksgiving. Tonight here, representing vaster audiences and greater forces moving outside this hall, it is both British and American thanksgiving that we may celebrate. And why is that? It is because under the compulsion of mysterious and allpowerful destiny we are together. We are joined together, shedding our blood side by side, struggling for the same ideals, until the triumph of the great causes which we serve shall have been made manifest.

But there is a greater Thanksgiving Day which still shines ahead, which beckons the bold and loyal and warm-hearted. And that is when this union of action which has been forced upon us by our common hatred of tyranny, which we have maintained during these dark and fearful days, shall become a lasting union of sympathy and good-feeling and loyalty and hope between all the British and American peoples, wherever they may dwell. Then, indeed, there will be a Day of Thanksgiving, and one in which all the world will share.

WINSTON S. CHURCHILL

CHAPTER 24| JFK'S FINAL PROCLAMATION

JOHN F KENNEDY #35

One of the Final actions taken by President Kennedy before his Assassination was to deliver this Thanksgiving Address. This portrait is by Norman Rockwell.

November 05, 1963

By the President of the United States of America

A Proclamation

Over three centuries ago, our forefathers in Virginia and in Massachusetts, far from home in a lonely wilderness, set aside a time of thanksgiving. On the appointed day, they gave reverent thanks for their safety, for the health of their children, for the fertility of their fields, for the love which bound them together and for the faith which united them with their God.

So too when the colonies achieved their independence, our first President in the first year of his first Administration proclaimed November 26, 1789, as "a day of public thanksgiving and prayer to be observed by acknowledging with grateful hearts the many signal favors of Almighty God" and called upon the people of the new republic to "beseech Him to pardon our national and other transgressions... to promote the knowledge and practice of true religion and virtue . . . and generally to grant unto all mankind such a degree of temporal prosperity as He alone knows to be best."

And so too, in the midst of America's tragic civil war, President Lincoln proclaimed the last Thursday of November 1863 as a day to renew our gratitude for America's "fruitful fields," for our "national strength and vigor," and for all our "singular deliverances and blessings."

Much time has passed since the first colonists came to rocky shores and dark forests of an unknown continent, much time since President

Washington led a young people into the experience of nationhood, much time since President Lincoln saw the American nation through the ordeal of fraternal war--and in these years our population, our plenty and our power have all grown apace. Today we are a nation of nearly two hundred million souls, stretching from coast to coast, on into the Pacific and north toward the Arctic, a nation enjoying the fruits of an ever-expanding agriculture and industry and achieving standards of living unknown in previous history. We give our humble thanks for this.

Yet, as our power has grown, so has our peril. Today we give our thanks, most of all, for the ideals of honor and faith we inherit from our forefathers--for the decency of purpose, steadfastness of resolve and strength of will, for the courage and the humility, which they possessed and which we must seek every day to emulate. As we express our gratitude, we must never forget that the highest appreciation is not to utter words but to live by them.

Let us therefore proclaim our gratitude to Providence for manifold blessings--let us be humbly thankful for inherited ideals--and let us resolve to share those blessings and those ideals with our fellow human beings throughout the world.

Now, Therefore, I, John F. Kennedy, President of the United States of America, in consonance with the joint resolution of the Congress approved December 26, 1941, 55 Stat. 862 (5 U.S.C. 87b), designating the fourth Thursday of November in each year as Thanksgiving Day, do hereby proclaim Thursday, November 28, 1963, as a day of national thanksgiving.

On that day let us gather in sanctuaries dedicated to worship and in homes blessed by family affection to express our gratitude for the glorious gifts of God; and let us earnestly and humbly pray that He will continue to guide and sustain us in the great unfinished tasks of achieving peace, justice, and understanding among all men and nations and of ending misery and suffering wherever they exist. *In Witness Whereof,* I have hereunto set my hand and caused the Seal of the United States of America to be affixed.

DONE at the City of Washington this fourth day of November, in the year of our Lord nineteen hundred and sixty-three, and of the Independence of the United States of America the one hundred and eighty-eighth.

JOHN F. KENNEDY
By the President:

CHAPTER 25 | PRESIDENT-ELECT JOE BIDEN

J oe Biden gave a Thanksgiving speech as president-elect shortly after winning the 2020 election. With a nod to the harsh divisions and difficult circumstances that compelled Washington and Lincoln to make their Thanksgiving Proclamations, Biden acknowledges the toll of the COVID-19 virus and hardened political divisions. When he states "America is a nation not of adversaries, but of neighbors." he is attempting to unite a fractured populace. When he say "First, let us be thankful for democracy itself." he extols the American democratic tradition with a tacit assertion that it is being threatened. #45's "big lie" and January 6 provocation to storm the Capitol are just ahead. It is a singular document at a pivotal moment in our history.

My fellow Americans:

Thanksgiving is a special time in America. A time to reflect on what the year has brought, and to think about what lies ahead.

The first national day of Thanksgiving, authorized by the Continental Congress, took place on December 18th, 1777. It was celebrated by General George Washington and his troops at Gulph Mills on the way to Valley Forge. It took place under harsh conditions and deprivations — lacking food, clothing, shelter. They were preparing to ride out a long hard winter.

Today, you can find a plaque in Gulph Mills marking that moment. It reads in part — "This Thanksgiving in spite of the suffering-showed the reverence and character that was forging the soul of a nation."

Forging the soul of a nation. Faith, courage, sacrifice, service to country, service to each other, and gratitude even in the face of suffering, have long been part of what Thanksgiving means in America. Looking back over our history you'll see that it's been in the most difficult of circumstances that the soul of our nation has been forged.

Now, we find ourselves again facing a long, hard winter. We have fought a nearly year-long battle with a virus in this nation. It's brought us pain and loss and frustration, and it has cost so many lives. 260,000 Americans — and counting. It has divided us. Angered us. And set us against one another.

I know the country has grown weary of the fight. But we need to remember we're at a war with a virus — not with each other. This is the moment where we need to steel our spines, redouble our efforts, and recommit ourselves to the fight.

Let's remember — we are all in this together. For so many of us, it's hard to hear that this fight isn't over, that we still have months of this battle ahead of us. And for those who have lost loved ones, I know this time of year is especially difficult.

Believe me, I know. I remember that first Thanksgiving. The empty chair, the silence. It takes your breath away. It's hard to care. It's hard to give thanks. It's hard to look forward.

And it's so hard to hope. I understand. I will be thinking and praying for each and every one of you at our Thanksgiving table because we've been there.

This year, we're asking Americans to forego many of the traditions that have long made this holiday such a special one.

For our family, we've had a 40 plus year tradition of traveling over Thanksgiving, a tradition we've kept every year save one — the year after our son Beau died.

But this year, we'll be staying home. We have always had big family gatherings at Thanksgiving. Kids, grand kids, aunts, uncles, and more. For the Bidens, the days around Thanksgiving have always been a time to remember all we had to be grateful for, and a time to welcome the Christmas Season.

But this year, because we care so much for each other, we're going to be having separate Thanksgivings. For Jill and I, we'll be at home in Delaware with our daughter and son-in-law. So, I know. I know how hard it is to forego family traditions, but it is so very important.

Our country is in the middle of a dramatic spike in cases. We're now averaging over 160,000 new cases a day. And no one will be surprised if we hit 200,000 cases in a single day. Many local health systems are at risk of being overwhelmed.

That is the plain and simple truth, and I believe you deserve to always hear the truth from your president.

We have to try to slow the growth of the virus. We owe that to the doctors, the nurses, and the other front-line health care workers who have risked so much and heroically battled this virus for so long.

We owe that to our fellow citizens who will need access to hospital beds and the care to fight this disease. And we owe it to one another — it's our patriotic duty as Americans. That means wearing masks, keeping social distancing, and limiting the size of any groups we're in. Until we have a vaccine, these are our most effective tools to combat the virus.

Starting on Day One of my presidency, we will take steps that will change the course of the disease. More testing will find people with cases and get them away from other people, slowing the number of infections. More protective gear for businesses and schools will do the same — reducing the number of cases. Clear guidance will get more businesses and more schools open. We all have a role to play in beating this crisis. The federal government has vast powers to combat this virus. And I commit to you I will use all those powers to lead a national coordinated response.

But the federal government can't do it alone. Each of us has a responsibility in our own lives to do what we can to slow the virus. Every decision we make matters. Every decision we make can save a life. None of these steps we're asking people to take are political statements. Every one of them is based in science.

The good news is, that there has been significant, record-breaking progress made recently in developing a vaccine. Several of these vaccines look to be extraordinarily effective. And it appears that we are on track for the first immunizations to begin by late December or early January. Then, we will need to put in place a distribution plan to get the entire country immunized as soon as possible, which we will do. But it's going to take time.

I'm hoping the news of a vaccine will serve as an incentive to every American to take these simple steps to get control of this virus.

There is real hope, tangible hope. So hang on. Don't let yourself surrender to the fatigue. I know we can and we will beat this virus. America is not going to lose this war. You will get your lives back. Life is going to return to normal. That will happen. This will not last forever.

So yes, this has been a hard year, but I still believe we have much to be thankful for. Much to hope for. Much to build upon. Much to dream of. Here's the America I see, and I believe it's the America you see, too:

An America that faces facts. An America that overcomes challenges. An America where we seek justice and equality for all people.

An America that holds fast to the conviction that out of pain comes possibility; out of frustration, progress; out of division, unity.

In our finest hours, that's who we've always been, and it's who we shall be again, for I believe that this grim season of division and demonization will give way to a year of light and unity.

Why do I think so?

Because America is a nation not of adversaries, but of neighbors. Not of limitation, but of possibility. Not of dreams deferred, but of dreams realized. I've said it many times: This is a great country and we are a good people.

This is the United States of America.

And there has never been anything we haven't been able to do when we've done it together.

Think of what we've come through: centuries of human enslavement; a cataclysmic Civil War; the exclusion of women from the ballot box; World Wars; Jim Crow; a long twilight struggle against Soviet tyranny that could have ended not with the fall of the Berlin Wall, but in nuclear Armageddon.

I'm not naïve. I know that history is just that: history. But to know what's come before can help arm us against despair. Knowing the previous generations got through the same universal human challenges that we face: the tension between selfishness and generosity, between fear and hope, between division and unity. And what was it that brought the reality of America into closer alignment with its promise of equality, justice, and prosperity?

It was love. Plain and simple. Love of country and love for one another. We don't talk much about love in our politics. The public arena is too loud, too angry, too heated.

To love our neighbors as ourselves is a radical act, yet it's what we're called to do. And we must try, for only in trying, only in listening, only in seeing ourselves as bound together in what Dr. King called a "mutual garment of destiny" can we rise above our divisions and truly heal.

America has never been perfect. But we've always tried to fulfill the aspiration of the Declaration of Independence: that all people are created equal, created in the image of God. And we have always sought "to form that more perfect union."

What should we give thanks for in this season?

First, let us be thankful for democracy itself. In this election year, we have seen record numbers of Americans exercise their most sacred right — that of the vote — to register their will at the ballot box.

Think about that. In the middle of a pandemic, more people voted this year than have ever voted in the history of America. Over 150 million people cast a ballot. That is simply extraordinary.

If you want to know what beats deep in the heart of America, it's this: democracy. The right to determine our lives, our government, our leaders. The right to be heard. Our democracy was tested this year. And what we learned is this: The people of this nation are up to the task.

In America, we have full and fair and free elections, and then we honor the results. The people of this nation and the laws of the land won't stand for anything else.

Through the vote — the noblest instrument of nonviolent protest ever conceived — we are reminded anew that progress is possible.

That "We the People" have the power to change what Jefferson called "the course of human events."

That with our hearts and hands and voices, today can be better than yesterday, and tomorrow can be better still.

We should be thankful, too, that America is a covenant and an unfolding story.

We have what we need to create prosperity, opportunity and justice: Americans have grit and generosity, a capacity for greatness and reservoirs of goodness.

We have what it takes. Now we must act. And this is our moment — ours together — to write a newer, bolder, more compassionate chapter in the life of our nation. The work ahead will not be easy. And it will not be quick.

You want solutions, not shouting. Reason, not hyper-partisanship. Light, not heat.

You want us to hear one another again, see one another again, and respect one another again. You want us — Democrats and Republicans and Independents — to come together and work together. And that, my friends, is what I am determined to do.

Americans dream big.

And, as hard as it may seem this Thanksgiving, we are going to dream big again. Our future is bright.

In fact, I have never been more optimistic about the future of America than I am right now. I believe the 21st Century is going to be an American Century. We are going to build an economy that leads the world.

We are going to lead the world by the power of our example — not the example of our power. We are going to lead the world on climate and save the planet. We are going to find cures for cancer and Alzheimer's and diabetes. And we are going to finally root out systemic racism in our country.

On this Thanksgiving, and in anticipation of all the Thanksgivings to come, let us dream again. Let us commit ourselves to thinking not only of ourselves but of others. For if we care for one another — if we open our arms rather than brandish our fists — we can, with God's help, heal. And if we do, and I am sure we can, we can proclaim with the Psalmist who wrote: "The Lord is my strength and my shield ... and with my song I give thanks to him."

And I give thanks now: for you and for the trust you have placed in me.

Together, we will lift our voices in the coming months and years, and our song shall be of lives saved, breaches repaired, and a nation made whole.

From the Biden family to yours, wherever and however you may be celebrating, we wish you a Happy Thanksgiving.

God bless you, and may God protect our troops.

Joseph R. Biden Jr. President-Elect

This is a singular document in that it shows Biden's plans for his administration, including a federal program regarding COVID-19. It is the state of our Nation prior to the Insurrection.

As of this writing it is not entirely clear how the brazen attack on democracy will play out. Prognosticating a worst case scenario regarding Trump is generally an exercise in wondering "Well, how bad could it be?" and being under served by one's imagination. Relying on civic institutions, democratic norms established over 250 years or cooler heads has been a cause for consternation. May Providence smile broadly upon Joe Biden when he states:

"Together, we will lift our voices in the coming months and years, and our song shall be of lives saved, breaches repaired, and a nation made whole."

The texts for all Presidential Proclamations can be located on the website The American Presidency Project at UC Santa Barbara.

(Proclamations: The American Presidency Project.) https://www.presidency.ucsb.edu